The Apprentice Leader

Learning to Serve a Senior Leader

Andrew Fox

Sovereign World

Sovereign World Ltd
PO Box 777
Tonbridge
Kent TN11 0ZS
England

Unless otherwise stated all Scripture quotations are taken from the
HOLY BIBLE, NEW INTERNATIONAL VERSION. Copyright © 1973,
1978, 1984 by International Bible Society. Used by permission.

New King James Version, copyright © 1983 by Thomas Nelson, Inc.

ISBN 1 85240 258 X

This Sovereign World book is distributed in North America by Renew
Books, a ministry of Gospel Light, Ventura, California, USA. For a free
catalog of resources from Renew Books/Gospel Light, please contact your
Christian supplier or call 1-800-4-GOSPEL.

Typeset by CRB Associates, Reepham, Norfolk.
Printed in the United States of America

Contents

	Preface	5
	Foreword	7
	Introduction	9
Chapter 1	The Foundation to Serve	13
Chapter 2	Four Questions	19
Chapter 3	The Danger of Inexperience	24
Chapter 4	Understanding Anointing and Personality	30
Chapter 5	Boundary Stones of Doctrine	34
Chapter 6	Different Personalities but the Same Spirit	39
Chapter 7	'That Which I Pass on to You'	44
Chapter 8	What About My Wife?	52
Chapter 9	Your Salary and His	59
Chapter 10	When it's Time to Leave	63
Chapter 11	Are You Strong Enough?	69
Chapter 12	The Apostle and the Apprentice	77
Chapter 13	Giving a Bride Away	83
Chapter 14	From Generation to Generation	90
Chapter 15	Defeating Intimidation	95
Chapter 16	Staying Focused for the Task	100

Chapter 17 The Last Adam, Not the First   104

A Review   108

Appendix   Questions with Answers from
Key Leaders   110

Preface

Andrew Fox is a well-respected young man who holds ministerial status with Assemblies of God in Great Britain and Ireland, and the United States. His early ministry was developed during a five-year period under the guidance of Brian Downward his senior minister. His first post as leader was at the Mid Devon Christian Center in Tiverton, England. In the summer of 1999 he accepted the position of Senior Minister at the First Assembly of God Church, Kennewick, Washington, USA. His ministry has influenced many churches in the West of England and gained acclaim from ministers overseas.

The book that Andrew has written is a relevant one. It arrives at a time when the young would rather divorce themselves from earlier generations. Andrew rightly counteracts this trend by showing the wisdom of being mentored by a senior minister.

As well as his own experience with a mentor, Andrew has also researched this important subject. The following pages contain practical, honest and biblical conclusions on such subjects as motivation, sacrifice, relationships, popularity, and finding the right wife, to mention but a few.

During the sixties, it was my privilege to be mentored for five years by Clyde Young, an Executive Member of the Assemblies of God. As I read the book, it brought back to me many precious memories and emotions. It also challenged my present position as a senior minister to continue mentoring younger men.

I would recommend this practical book both to young ministers who would seek the wisdom and counsel of a senior man of God, and to those who have matured, and would seek to father the young-developing minister

Paul C. Weaver
General Superintendent
Assemblies of God in Great Britain and Ireland

Foreword

Sitting with a gifted leader in his early 30s I asked some direct questions about his call to Christ and ministry, reflected with him about his gifts and some areas where he needed to show stronger leadership. It was important to encourage him – it always is – and try to answer honestly some of his questions. After about twenty minutes he said, 'Why has this never happened before? I know a number of senior leaders but none of them has ever spoken to me like this.' This is a true story. I could repeat it with varying details many times over. The implications of this both delight and horrify me. The Bible says that there are many who would be teachers, but not many who are prepared to be fathers. Oh for more fathers – men with potent and passionate spirituality that can give birth to equally productive sons.

If an apprentice leader is to reach his potential, effectively and efficiently, then some craftsmen must first invest their time, love and skill into the young man's development. It is good to give people an opportunity in ministry, but much better to make disciples. It is good to be able to recognize gifting, but much better to help shape it. It is good to 'succeed' in your own ministry, but much better to be vulnerable, available to mentor, empower and help the next generation to climb higher, run faster, see further and achieve more. Genesis 48:16 tells us that when Israel blessed Joseph he said,

> 'May the God ... who has been my shepherd all my life to this day, the Angel who has delivered me from all harm –

> **may he bless these boys** ... *may they increase greatly upon the earth.'*

So be it, Lord.

In this much-needed and very practical book, Andrew Fox presents the challenges and opportunities, pitfalls and potential of serving a senior leader, and explains how growing in this fertile environment will prepare you for a strong healthy leadership. It is my prayer that the excellent work he has done, assisted by one of my own spiritual sons, Tim Pettingale, and presented in the following pages, will help both the apprentice and the craftsman in their journey of advancing the greatest Father and Son business in the universe. The world needs well prepared, properly fathered leaders. I am hopeful that this book will be a stimulus to many on their journey.

> **David Shearman**
> Nottingham
> September 1999

Introduction

Have you ever had an alarmingly realistic dream and then been totally unable to explain the episode upon waking? Have you ever woken in a cold sweat, gradually emerging from a make-believe world to the real one, having been held between the conscious and the unconscious with no beginning and no end? I'm sure all of us have. A scientific study has proven that, although dreams seem to last for hours at a time, the maximum a person will actually dream for is just ten minutes, and that short sequence repeats itself over and over again. Just one hour after falling asleep, an observer would see your eyeballs moving frantically beneath closed lids as though your brain was receiving visual images. Your body may also begin to react physically, probably to the detriment of whoever happened to be sleeping next to you!

The Bible has quite a lot to say about dreams. God has often used them as an effective way to communicate with His servants. 'Dreams' is also the phrase we use to describe the indescribable – deep seated feelings, desires, emotions, longings – call them what you will, whatever name we give to them, our inner dreams are like reflections of our God-given destiny and purpose. Every one of us has dreams we would like to fulfil. Some have great dreams of achieving great things, but in order for them to become a reality, a very practical process has to take place. It involves commitment, hard work and determination. Making your dreams come true is not as easy as it seems!

Many zealous and gifted young men who have given their lives to Christ, dream of becoming great men of God, great leaders leading great churches, accomplishing great things for God. No one can teach greatness, and I'm certainly not going to try! But, if you desire to become a leader of quality, integrity and humility – read on. Countless key leaders have discovered the joy of being mentored and discipled by godly men who have walked in the way before them and learnt their own valuable lessons. You may be a trail blazing pioneer, full of innovative ideas and energy, but let me suggest to you that however high you think you can climb now, you will reach further than you imagined with the help of an experienced instructor. I have learnt countless lessons by serving a senior leader. I didn't have to do it that way, but I am grateful to God that He allowed me to be prepared for leadership by serving, observing, gradually branching out myself, making mistakes, learning and growing, steadily building spiritual muscle.

The Bible gives us several examples to study in terms of spiritual sons and fathers. Eli was a spiritual father to Samuel (1 Samuel 3:6); Paul was a spiritual father to Timothy (1 Timothy 1:2) and also Titus and Onesimus; Elisha called Elijah 'father' (2 Kings 2:12). In this book we will explore how such a relationship might work in practice. My desire is that for many, it will help the substance of young dreams – the dreams of young men who desire to devote their lives to serving the Body of Christ – to be brought into reality by first serving a senior leader. Barney Coombs in his book, *Apostles Today* has this to say,

> '...fathers are relatively few in number, and in an age where fatherhood has been all but lost, there is a desperate need for such men to be recognized and received. For instance, there are many men pastoring churches today who themselves have never been fathered – either by their natural fathers or any spiritual fathers. Such men tend to be insecure, and for that reason are usually defensive when offered well-meaning advice or (in some cases) well-deserved criticism.'[1]

We must resist becoming unteachable at every stage of our lives, even when we are experienced. A spiritual mentor can help us in this. Coombs continues,

> …having a mentor will always be more effective in someone's formation than just receiving **information** … Mentoring can find its best expression in the Church, where the quality of relationship and significance of mission are at their highest potential level.'[2]

There are clear markings in a man that make a him a leader. An artist or a musician may produce fine work and by default attract a following, indirectly influencing people – sometimes stimulating and sometimes agitating them – but this is not leadership. A person may have a clear vision to accomplish some work, but unless they enthuse and inspire others, motivating them to work towards it with them, that is not leadership either.

A leader shares a common goal with those who follow him. He behaves in a manner that influences them. He has a character that can withstand difficult times as well as good, and possesses a personality that draws people to him. His authority does not need to 'shout', but most of all his anointing is recognized by those who follow him. Such skills are best learned while serving another man's ministry.

Once, a man was sitting in a train carriage with six other passengers. He had two children with him who were running up and down the passage-way making a great deal of noise as they played. The other passengers became increasingly angered by this man who would do nothing to stop his children. Eventually, a young man who was in the carriage stood up and confronted him telling him what he should do. He looked up at the young man and explained, 'I have come from the hospital where their mother has just died of cancer and I don't know how to tell them.' Immediately the young man's temperament was changed.

The young and headstrong often rush into situations believing that they alone have the solution. However, a mentor may bring directional thinking into your life that will change your view on what ministry is and what it is not. He can often detect the story behind the story before the facts become evident. Serving a senior man can help you to turn your dream into an effective ministry that neither merely stimulates nor agitates a body of believers, but influences them with clear direction. Your dreams can live!

Meditate for a moment on the words of Solomon, and then we will begin our journey together:

> 'Hear, O sons, the instruction of a father,
> And give attention that you may gain understanding.
> For I give you sound teaching;
> Do not abandon my instruction.
> When I was a son of my father,
> Tender and the only son in the sight of my mother,
> Then he taught me and said to me,
> "Let your heart hold fast to my words;
> Keep my commandments and live;
> Acquire wisdom! Acquire understanding! . . ."
> Hear, my son, and accept my sayings,
> And the years of your life will be many.
> I have directed you in the way of wisdom;
> I have led you in upright paths.
> When you walk, your steps will not be impeded;
> And if you run, you will not stumble.
> Take hold of instruction; do not let it go.
> Guard her for she is your life.'   (Proverbs 4:1–13)

References

1. Coombs, Barney. *Apostles Today, Christ's Love-gift to the Church*, 1996, Sovereign World.

2. Ibid, p. 131.

Chapter 1

The Foundation to Serve

Before entering into any aspect of ministry there is a foundation to be laid in your heart that will provide a solid base for future building. It is very easy to listen to an experienced teacher and think, 'I could do that!' and totally miss the fact that what you are hearing is the result of years of preparation, character building and hard work. Maybe you could get up and preach the same message, but would it have the same authenticity and weight to it? Let me suggest to you that serving another man's ministry before being released into your own is pivotal in laying a solid foundation. It is cultivating the ability to allow your gift to die in order to live.

A prominent elderly leader once told me a simple truth that has protected the individual gifting and calling upon my life when serving other men. Allow me to quote him:

> 'When you reach a certain age you think that nothing can stop you. Then as you become middle-aged and realize that there is little time left, you see that younger men are catching up and going further. Finally you reach yet another age where you realize that it really doesn't matter any more. It becomes a pleasure to see others doing what you cannot do!'

If you desire **significance** rather than **success**, then you will realize the importance of learning from an older and more experienced person. When you stop learning, you stop growing. The journey begins for anyone called of God when they start serving another man's ministry. Usually that ministry will be approaching or already in the middle stage already mentioned.

Here is where the foundational work is laid in your heart. Like any building construction, the most important work will be unnoticed and probably unappreciated, but essential to the solid construction of the building and its long-term stability. In laying this foundation I have discovered several keys that will I believe will help you to keep a godly perspective on the sometimes painful process of allowing God to shape you and prepare you:

1. It only matters to you

'So Samuel took the horn of oil and anointed him in the presence of his brothers, and from that day on the Spirit of the Lord came upon David in power.'   (1 Samuel 16:13)

Let's examine that momentous event in the life of King David in the light of a modern church setting. A prophet comes to your church and begins to speak into the lives of the congregation with you sitting at the back seemingly uninterested. He then calls you to the front where everyone can see, lays hands on you and begins to speak prophetic utterances over you! All the leadership team are looking and listening, and the prophet has not yet ministered to them. God speaks things through the prophet about your life and destiny in Him that fill you with excitement. After the service a few old ladies encourage you sympathetically, but guess what, no-one from the leadership team seems to recognize that God has just confirmed His Word in you!

Well, that's exactly what happened to David while he was tending his sheep. Following on from that event we find him going down to the battlefield when Israel has a problem with Goliath. On his arrival perhaps his brothers should have recognized the fact that he had the call of God and an anointing to do what they could not do. Instead we read:

'I know how conceited you are and how wicked your heart is; you came down only to watch the battle.'

(1 Samuel 17:28b)

Understand this, that in the laying of the foundation no-one really gets excited about the prospect of the finished piece of architecture except you! Nothing of faith and possibility came over David's brothers – only ridicule. Now what would your reaction be? Probably varied, but certainly a feeling of hurt and rejection. If you can accept that in all the circumstances of life God is mostly concerned with shaping your character – forming Christ in you – then you will realize that at times like these God is digging up another part of you to make a foundation that will build greatness in you.

2. Nothing changes

'But David went back and forth from Saul to tend his fathers sheep at Bethlehem.' (1 Samuel 17:15)

Again, let's put that in the modern church setting. The leadership of your local church seems to treat you exactly as it always has, even though you feel God has put the future in your heart. It is not that the present leadership are wrong or failing to hear from God, but you are in a state of preparation. God may well have in mind that He is preparing you to advance the vision, but it is not yet time for you to assume that office – there's a lot of work to be done yet! In a self-examination, you will see one key element that the leadership have and you don't. It is the very element that Paul seems to stress in every chapter to his protégé Timothy – wisdom. It takes a very humble man to hold the future in his heart and yet keep tending sheep, especially when he longs to be at the helm of a great church, steering it through the storms and currents of a spiritual battle. You long to bring a new sphere of worship to the church, deepen the presence of God in the life of the people, win more battles than any predecessor and increase the vision to its fullness, yet still you remain working at the factory, office or building site. Nothing seems to change around you except you. However, if you can look at tending sheep as part of the call God has placed upon you, another piece will be dug out of you for a strong foundation.

3. Keep a right attitude

In 1 Kings chapter 19 we read of how Elijah passed by Elisha working in the field and threw his mantle upon him. He knew in his heart that this man was to be his successor. The passing of the mantle was symbolic of Elisha's election to receive the authority and power of his office.

> *'He [Elisha] took his yoke of oxen and slaughtered them. He burned the ploughing equipment to cook the meat and gave it to the people, and they ate. Then he set out to follow Elijah and became his attendant.'*   (1 Kings 19:21)

The only person to change here was Elisha. He no longer farmed his land and worked the plough but became a servant of Elijah. The future of Elisha was to be spectacular, but his present schooling was to be one of attending another man.

2 Kings 2:15b says, *'The spirit of Elijah is resting upon Elisha.'* If you were to read the text between these two passages of scripture and try to map out what Elisha really did, you would struggle, but the Bible is full of 'loaded' statements and expressions that require some reading between the lines to appreciate the bigger picture. The giveaway here is the last word of the first scripture: attendant. Because Elisha was prepared to be nothing more than a servant, he eventually found himself anointed by God and in the leading role – the attendant had become the prophet. If Elijah ever needed something Elisha ran to get it for him. Elisha even addressed Elijah as 'My father! My father!' (2 Kings 2:12b). Trust, respect, and sincerity had been built up between Elijah and Elisha that caused a unique attitude in the one serving. The reality is that Elijah did not have to change but Elisha did. To lead is to serve and to serve is to lead.

From all of this we may conclude that your spirit has to be the kind that does not quit easily. Robert Schuller said that every morning when we wash, all the negative thoughts should be 'rinsed out'. Then, according to Schuller, we are to use a 'mental detector' to trace anything that is still left behind and deal with it. If you quit at the start the potential you could have reached will never be realized.

Did you hear about the world's largest bell that has never yet been rung? It was commissioned by the Tzar of Russia, weighed 219 tons and stood 18 feet high. During its construction a fire broke out in the foundry and a single drop of water got into the mould as workers fought vigorously to put out the flames. When the bell was cast it cracked because of that one drop of water and so has never been heard.

How many have been 'called' but have failed to be 'chosen' because of an unteachable spirit that cracked the mould of what would have been a tremendous ministry bringing glory to God? Being moulded may not be an altogether pleasant experience, but quitting is the only thing that can stop you finishing – because finishing, by definition, means that at least you made it! Never quit – carry on! Look at the following historic examples:

Thomas Edison failed in so many inventions that the rubble thrown out of his office window reached the second floor! He sent men to Japan, South America, Asia, and Jamaica looking for an element that would withstand the power of electricity running through a new invention called the light bulb. On 21 October 1879 after 13 months of trying he found what was needed only to face another set of problems. He could not manage to fix it in place within a vacuum sealed unit. After two days and nights of trying he finally succeeded, making an almost poetic statement: 'The sight we so longed to see finally met our eyes.'

Imagine the demonic host looking at you, desperate to crack the great mould and enjoy seeing the failure of humanity represented in the natural state of your being – depressing isn't it! Now look towards the Father and hear His son speaking to Him on your behalf, stating that He has every confidence that through Him you can make it, or in other words: 'Father, the sight we so longed to see in this man will eventually meet our eyes!'

The Beatles were turned down by the HMV, Columbia and Decca record companies who thought that the 'boy band with guitars' era was over. Paul McCartney once wrote a song that went, 'Scrambled eggs, Oh my baby how I love your legs'! With a lot of work it became, 'Yesterday, all my troubles seemed so far away'. In 1995 McCartney was interviewed about the beginnings of what became a defined part of British musical culture. He stated: 'We just would not quit.'

Charles Darrow was an engineer in the great depression of America 1932. He invented a game that Parker Brothers found 52 faults in. For two years he worked at perfecting given faults in the game that would make you rich by the roll of a dice. That game is the best selling game in the world – Monopoly.

Colonel Sanders founded his fried chicken fast food chain at the age of 65. He would not let the fact that he was of retiring age dictate his usefulness to the commercial world.

Roger Bannister was told that it was scientifically impossible for a man to run a four-minute mile. After he broke that barrier thirty-seven other men did so within a year, and three hundred more the following year. It only takes one man to set the course for many men.

If you realize that the development of godly character in your life will not matter to anyone except **you**, and that nothing will change except **you**, and that you must have a **right attitude** that is teachable, then you will have made a good start on the journey to becoming a leader of distinction. It could be your name that goes down in history as a man who did something that lived longer than he did.

Chapter 2

Four Questions

In this chapter I want to ask four questions about serving a senior leader that will hopefully take away all the glamour of ministering to people and lead you back to the two most essential elements in your life – God's calling and anointing. I am sure there are many aspiring students who have observed well-known people and been attracted to their 'public position' in a vicarious way – in other words enjoying the thrill of being used mightily by God by observing their experiences and imagining them to be their own. In their mind they are preaching to a church who loves them and responds to every word uttered from their lips, who provide for all their needs in abundance, and respect their every decision. Well, although the thought of being in that place may bring a rush of adrenaline, it usually gives no hint of the pressure or responsibility that accompanies such a position. And what of the leader's apprentice who is often taking a back seat whilst his mentor goes about his ministry? Responding correctly to the pressures that this situation creates is a key to your effective preparation. Answer these questions for yourself:

1. Can you serve when you know you are meant to lead?

There are essentially two types of people: those who minister well when under another's covering, and those who minister well when operating in their own right. In either case you will only discover which type of person you are by serving another man. If the anointing of God is upon you to stand on your own two feet, there will come a time when the senior man recognizes that staying with him will do neither of you any good. However, if you are the type that ministers most effectively under his covering, then to leave him could be disastrous. Jesus had twelve men who served Him for three years, but the end product was considerably varied. Not all became prominent before the people as individual leaders with a unique anointing, some were referred to as a collective body, while others – like Peter, Philip, James, and later Paul – were singled out. Even Silas, Barnabas and John Mark were only effective whilst with Paul. Examine your own calling with honesty and integrity, and inevitably there will come a time when you discover where you fit in. Were you born to be a senior leader or a supporting team member? Trying to be a senior leader when you are really a supporting player can be damaging and exhausting. Being a potential senior leader locked into a supporting role is equally frustrating and crushing. However, to know your calling, place and function is liberating, rewarding and fulfilling. What if you realize you are destined to lead in your own right? In this growing and learning period you will find yourself having to serve – everyone does. Don't think of it as holding you back, but rather holding you in. God is simply preparing you and shaping your character.

2. Can you serve and remain unrecognized?

Former President George Bush once went to visit a rest home for the elderly and was filmed in the usual way since it was during election time. The camera focused upon him holding an old lady's hand as he asked: 'Do you know who I am?' She responded in a matter of fact way, 'No, but if you ask at reception I am sure they will be able to help you!' Everyone wants recognition from others, but how often we fail to understand the obvious: the only recognition we will get is from those who **do** recognize us!

A prominent evangelist came with his team to the church I served in. One of his team was booked to come back at a later date during the summer months. During his visit the evangelist drew a packed congregation, whereas his team member drew a crowd less than an eighth as large. Why? One could put it down to bad planning, lack of publicity, the wrong day of the week – but viewing the event as a whole, the obvious conclusion was drawn: 'No one recognized the team member in the same way they recognized his leader.' Why is 'recognition' in this context so important anyway? Because it is the **anointing** on you that people are drawn to. Jesus only had to be talking casually to His disciples and a crowd would follow.

In 1 Samuel 16:23 we read that David regularly ministered to King Saul, who has being oppressed by an evil spirit:

> *'David would take his harp and play. Then relief would come to Saul; he would feel better, and the evil spirit would leave him.'*

One might draw the conclusion from this passage that if David ministered on his harp within the tents of King Saul, that he was 'known' by Saul. But that is far from the truth. After David had gone out to kill Goliath and Israel rejoiced, both Abner – a senior officer – and Saul himself, failed to recognize who this champion was.

> *' "Abner, whose son is that young man?" Abner replied, "As surely as you live, O king, I don't know." The King said, "Find out whose son this young man is." '*
>
> (1 Samuel 17:55b–56)

In serving another man there will be times when you surpass him and yet remain 'unknown'. Following on from this event, David must soon have become known to many, but also be aware that before you begin slaying giants yourself, any recognition you receive will be largely due to you being under your leader's covering – the profile and privileges are yours because of him!

3. Can you cope with the senior man's prosperity while you scrape around?

One of the three major things that have the potential to ruin a man at any stage of his ministry is money – the other two being sex and power. In the West we are immersed in a culture that evaluates our life by the type of car we drive or the property we live in. There are many biblical truths that speak of God prospering a man who fears and obeys Him, giving him the wealth of the world. We are quick to notice the many blessing God has given to someone else, but it is often easy to fail to see the road that led to this state of plenty. If there is one signpost that consistently appears on that road it is 'Obedience rather than sacrifice'. As Moses was obedient to God he received all he needed to build the tabernacle from Egypt. Solomon received all he needed and more to construct a temple for the Lord. When your spiritual compass is set to the right values, it will not be the car you drive or the house you live in that evaluates your worth, but the anointing upon you. As Peter and John found,

> ' "*Silver or gold I do not have, but what I have I give you.*" '
> (Acts 3:6)

It is particularly in the area of financial well-being that your real motives for ministry become apparent to yourself (and more especially to others), and the validity of your calling is proven. If your values are higher than income and possession, then during times of famine as well as prosperity, your values will still hold their power. Is the divine call of your Creator worth more in value to you than the rewards of being obedient to that call? The Apostle Paul spoke about his experiences of material things – sometimes having plenty and sometimes very little, yet remaining content with either state of affairs. Even if it seems to you that your mentor is quite prosperous and you are on the breadline, don't despair! Learn to be content and grateful for what you have, it will teach you to be a good steward of the resources God has given you. God knows your needs, so trust Him to meet them.

4. Can you keep a confidence with integrity?

There were many times when Jesus withdrew with His disciples to teach them the deeper things of God, and more so the three that were closest to Him – Peter, James and John.

It affected their ministry and gave them a deeper and more comprehensive understanding of the things of God, compared to the narrow thinking of their contemporaries.

To hear any news, be it good or bad, that is exclusive or confidential is always exciting because it brings with it a sense of power. But with the insight into confidentiality comes increased responsibility – to be aware of not using what you know about people in an adverse way, or for your own advantage. There is a school of dangerous 'word giving' in the Church – i.e. speaking prophetic utterances into a person's life that amount to little more than a simple summary of careful observation and inside knowledge about a situation. Likewise, while praying for an individual publicly, the confidential things that you know through your relationship with the senior leader, can easily come out as if they were words of revelation and knowledge, when it is really an abuse of confidence.

1 Peter 2:16 says, '...*do not use your freedom as a cover up for evil*...' 'Evil' is a very strong word, and I do not wish to focus on that part of the above text. Suffice it to say that the expression 'cover up' – carrying the literal meaning of 'throwing a cloak over to cover maliciousness' is the real focus here. The expression is the same one used for the outer cover of the Tabernacle – the part that all men see while the inside remains hidden. A young man can use his freedom of partnership with the senior man, all be it a subordinate one, as a cover for shallowness of doctrine and holiness, concealing a private life behind the scenes that is far short of the ideal.

Above all, remain teachable. If there is any imbalance in your ministry, the one you serve will take you to task over it, but it will be entirely up to you as to how you receive and disseminate his counsel. If a man was drowning twenty feet away from your boat and you threw him a fifteen foot rope, an observer might say that you went more than half way to saving the man! But if he drowned what was achieved? In other words, listen to your mentor. Allow him to impart the life-saving words that will help to ground your ministry. That is the unique and priceless advantage of serving another man – lessons are learned and grafted into your spirit far quicker, as long as you are prepared to take it.

Chapter 3

The Danger of Inexperience

The purpose for your life and ministry, implanted in you by God, will produce a passion in you that longs to achieve it. If that passion has no directive from experience then it will become destructive. Of course the only way to gain experience is by actually doing the job, but there must be parameters, and there must be accountability. In a court of law there is a category of offences labeled 'Crimes of Passion' – in other words, acts that were not premeditated but were carried out on impulse without prior thought. Many 'crimes' have been committed in ministry by zealous young men that were extremely well-intentioned, but ultimately misguided. Your senior leader should be the director of your passion under God – helping to shape and direct your enthusiasm in a constructive way. I have heard the phrase so many times – and always from mavericks and lone-rangers – 'I do not serve man, but God!' and generally speaking they fall into this category too – 'Criminals of passion'!

At least once a year, as a family, we will take a flight overseas for a break. With children it becomes more like a military operation than a comfortable journey! After boarding the plane, the captain will usually introduce himself and explain the details of the flight. If in that explanation he was heard saying, 'I have had a difficult week, but I will try my best to fly you to the destination' I would be the first to leave! If you are not passionate about the call of God upon your life then no-one is going to back you up. I am not saying that we should not be passionate and enthusiastic, merely that an appropriate expression of that passion is to be obedient in the place God has put you, and to learn from the experience and wisdom of others.

When working with someone who has already accomplished something of that which you are just starting to achieve, there is another danger to be aware of, that if not understood at the outset, can cause a great deal of hurt to both parties, that is idolizing your mentor. By way of example, allow me to put before you a real situation I have observed:

A young man starts out on his ministry with his eyes fixed on his senior leader or mentor, observing all he does whilst in and out of the pulpit. He learns quickly, soaking up every opportunity to gain the experience he needs. However, without even recognizing it, he becomes more and more absorbed in his pursuit, becoming ever more single-minded in it. All he talks about is the man he is serving. That young man may have a family who encouraged him to seek the Lord as he grew up through school and started his first job, or a youth pastor who stood by him. Suddenly they become obscured, and seemingly rejected as the mentor absorbs all the focused energy of that young and inexperienced man.

There is an important principle to be learned here: never forget your parents and those who helped you to get this far.

> *'Honor your father and mother ... and it will go well for you.'* (Exodus 20:12)

A senior man will never replace the affection and unconditional love and commitment of your own father. It shows a great deal of maturity when a young man can come home to his parents and still consider them to be the best teachers he has ever had. Often, quite the reverse can happen. The mentor becomes the repository of all knowledge for the young man and the advice of others is discarded, causing much hurt and feelings of rejection. Remember that he is only a man! Keep things in balance. Realize that first and foremost you personally are walking with God and He deserves the best of your time and attention, and secondly honor the family that God has given you. Never give them second-best.

The right motive

In Chapter 1 I wrote about the three stages of ministerial life. Let me remind you:

> ...then you get to middle age and realize there is little time left as the younger men catch up and go further...'

It is highly probable that as you assume your first 'assignment' as a young minister that the man you serve will be in this middle stage of ministry, realizing that time is not on his side, and there are not that many energetic years left where his physical and mental abilities will be at their sharpest. This will present a number of conflicts between you both. He will possess the wisdom and experience, and you will possess the energy and mental agility.

Once you get through the stage of seeing the senior man as the 'one and only' realizing that those close to you who love you probably did more, this area of conflict is usually the next bridge to cross. The 'conflict' manifests itself in numerous misunderstandings of motive – usually existing only in the mind. Because you are both at different stages in your ministry cycle, it is easy to question one another's motives and become hyper-critical.

For instance, it may seem at times as if your mentor is re-living his youth through you, but not making any allowance for your own individual choices. Of course, this will be 'from time to time', and not necessarily a constant pressure, but nevertheless it aggravates you. He may hold very strong ethical beliefs that he desires to keep to the letter, whereas you may be a little more liberal on a number of issues. His seeming pettiness irritates you. During this phase the pendulum may swing from one extreme to another as the slightest discrepancy you see in him becomes blown out of proportion in your unbalanced thinking, not allowing for the obvious – he is only human after all! All the time he may have done nothing wrong, nothing that is out of the ordinary in a relationship such as this, but in your eyes things are seen in a different way. He has used you, manipulated, dominated, and intimidated you the whole time!

This is where the danger of inexperience is perhaps manifest the greatest – in dealing with the unexpected pressures that relationships, particularly ones as intense as this, present to us. It is so easy to overreact and behave in an inappropriate way. Be prepared – this is one bridge that is long, very narrow and has many places where it is easy to fall off. Someone who feels like they are a victim is a dangerous person. All they see becomes clouded with a single issue that probably has little or nothing to do with the real issue at hand. Stay teachable with a right spirit and a right motive – not gullible, but quietly pursuing the experience you don't yet have.

One personality and one person

There is a great difference between a 'star' and a 'celebrity' in the world of entertainment and the arts. A celebrity has tremendous personality but no real genius, but a star always carries an air of importance with them because they are uniquely gifted, and everyone recognizes it. It might be that they have a superb voice, acting skills, or creativity that no-one else can match. Their genius protects them because the world needs them. Because they feel invaluable they can allow their attitude to be exactly how **they** determine, and not be influenced by how others think they **should** act in the public eye. If we adapt this principle to our thinking, we may draw several parallels.

I am not for a moment suggesting that the call of God is anything to do with entertainment, but I am making a parallel in personality. The senior man will probably have accomplished something in his life that denotes him as being a good man. It may be a church he planted that has grown and become a role model for other churches, or a Bible school he established that has become successful – something that makes him accomplished and forms part of his legacy. Generally, you only get one or two chances to do something powerful and lasting within one lifetime, so the senior man will probably be known for whatever it is he has done, even if it was a decade ago. To establish something like this would have taken the call and anointing of God, accompanied by much sacrifice. That in itself will have helped to make him the man he is. The younger man who comes along to serve him, however, may neglect to see the 'star' (the genius) in the senior man and try to imitate the 'celebrity' (personality) that he sees – wrongly attributing his success to this aspect of the man. The older man has credibility which the younger man seeks to trade off because he has none himself. Unless he takes a regular check on his own teachability, the chances of that young man developing into a 'star' himself are very small.

The example of Joseph

At the age of 17 Joseph began to dream. He saw a future in which his whole family bowed before him and became subservient to him. What he dreamt about was not wrong, but how he handled it was disastrous. He dashed straight out to inform them all how he would be as a king over them! Not only did he rouse the anger of his brothers, but also his father, Jacob. Consider also Jesus' disciples, James and John, who had their sights set on the places of honor to the right and left of Him in glory. They only saw a crown when Jesus spoke of the bitter cup, and only the throne when He spoke of the cross. A young man will always see the bright lights of publicity before he sees the pathway. Joseph saw the glory of his brothers bowing to him in his dreams of corn and stars, but failed to anticipate the accusation of Potiphar's wife, the slavery, the imprisonment, and the near death that would lead him to his destiny. An inexperienced man tried to keep Jesus from the cross – Peter. The same inexperienced man cut off the ear of a servant, and later swore and cursed when under pressure from a servant girl. Another inexperienced man tried to preach life when he had caused so much death – Paul in Jerusalem.

A soldier who has been serving his superiors for a few weeks will not know how to handle the weapons at his disposal correctly, just as a teenager who has just passed a driving test cannot quite handle motorways yet. So it is with an inexperienced man. He has the tools of the trade at his disposal, but will need his senior leader to keep a tight hold on the reigns for a while – not to hold him down, but to hold him in, and prevent disaster. Numerous biblical characters tell the same story. The anointing of God comes, then the training and preparation, then the full release. Go back and study your Bible again, and listen to the advice of David, Joshua, Gideon, Elisha and the rest. Be teachable, be wise, and learn all you can from those who have walked this way already.

Chapter 4

Understanding Anointing and Personality

As we have discovered, anyone seeking to develop into a significant leader under the covering of a senior leader, must be absolutely prepared for conflict. Maybe due to the fact that the younger man has held the senior man in too high esteem in his own thinking, every day minor conflicts become enlarged and viewed out of all proportion. Requests to bring the car around to the front of the church or lock up after everyone has gone home become a personal trial for the younger man – sometimes a sentence. It can begin to affect your ministry and development for greater things. What is more, people will see it sooner than you think. Let us examine one of the key factors in all of this: personality and character. How you react to the things that are happening to you is vastly more important than the things themselves. Just like the situation with Elijah and Elisha: **The senior man does not change but you must**.

Beware of a superficial perspective

Under the mature and developed anointing of God, the senior man may say and do things that at times seem outrageous. He will get away with it though, because of the anointing that is upon him. He may be building an ark in a time of drought like Noah, pouring water on an altar like Elijah, or sacrificing something dear to him like Abraham. To a young trainee it appears exciting because it is controversial, and he wrongly perceives it as being due to the man's personality – and tries to emulate it – when it is really due to the man's anointing, born out of his relationship with God.

It is important to recognize this truth. The attraction of 'controversy' may ruin years of steady growth, development and credibility. In a different context Peter experienced a similar circumstance with Simon who practised sorcery. Admittedly, Simon was not directly serving Peter as in our situation – but the principle of 'seeing only the surface' is very clear in this example.

> *'Now for some time a man named Simon had practised sorcery in the city and amazed all the people of Samaria. He boasted that he was someone great ... Simon himself believed and was baptized. And he followed Philip every-where, astonished by the great signs and miracles he saw ... When Simon saw that the Spirit was given at the laying on of the apostle's hands, he offered them money and said, "Give me also this ability so that everyone on whom I lay my hands may receive the Holy Spirit." But Peter said to him, "Your money perish with you, because you thought that the gift of God could be purchased with money! You have no part or share in this ministry, because your heart is not right before God."'*
> (Acts 8:9–21)

Simon had viewed the ministry of the apostles on an extremely superficial level. There are too many like Simon, who expect a 'quick-fix' from God that will enable them to minister as the senior man does. Did Simon consider the priceless time Peter had spent being rebuked by Jesus, learn-ing some hard lessons about what the Kingdom is and is not? No. He simply wanted what he saw.

Of course, I am not ruling out the instantaneous work of God through 'whosoever' – like the boy who offered his five loaves and two fish – because God can use anyone He chooses at any time to do whatever He wants. But never forget that Almighty God is using perishable, earthen, mortal, temporal vessels to carry His renowned name. That name is *'...majestic in all the earth...'* (Psalm 8:1), and will never become weakened or devalued according to the thinking of any vessel.

I would encourage any younger man serving a senior man to sit down, ask him questions, and listen to his response as to **how, when** and **where** he moves in such anointing, be it controversial or not. Find out the lessons, heartaches, failures, successes, and most of all the precious times of being alone with God listening to what He has to say. You will find that the difference between the ordinary man and the extraordinary man is in fact the little 'extra', and in all that will happen to you God will always do far more than you ever expected. The senior man will have cultivated this principle of truth in his spirit over time and hard-won experience.

Who gives out the orders?

Another key to survival as a training leader is the ability to identify when the senior leader's anointing is in action, and when it is just his personality operating. It is sometimes very difficult to know whether views he is expressing are tried and tested spiritual truths, or perhaps the product of his domestic situation. For example, how well do you get along with the senior leader's wife? Do you have a working, professional, personal, or distant relationship with her? You can be sure that on many occasions you are going to be in her house with her husband, and to make matters more challenging, it may well be that her children see less of their father than you do. This can be a major stress-point.

If the senior leader is under pressure from his family – and rightly so – to spend more time with them, when he is spending most of it with you, sometimes suppressed feelings can come rushing out when you least expect them. Maybe you have made a slight mistake that really needs no more than a frown to correct you, yet you receive a scolding rebuke. At that point you need the ability to separate the personality from the anointing and not confuse the two as being God's wrath against you when all along it is a result of domestic pressure.

Most senior men who have a track record of success, also have a wife that has far more underneath the surface than you would initially imagine! You have to be wise to understand and build on that. Your relationship with her could be either the greatest bonus or the greatest trial of your time spent serving that ministry.

If the senior man has children, you must also work hard to build clear boundaries of friendship with them. His children may well be of the same generation as you. Consequently, the level of respect they have for you may be something to work at! If he has sons they may see you as taking their place, potentially causing a great deal of jealousy. If this is the case, you must understand that this is not your problem but his, as the father of that family and the one who is responsible for providing their emotional stability and security as sons. But remain vigilant for such things and don't be ignorant of something that could work against you. If he has daughters, they may not feel invaded by your presence in their home as would his sons, but they will have feelings!

So be aware. Learn to separate the spiritual from the ordinary – the anointing from the personality. And in all your dealings remember, petty people are concerned with petty things and significant people are concerned with significant things. Keep a godly perspective.

Chapter 5

Boundary Stones of Doctrine

Proverbs 22:28 says,

> 'Do not remove an ancient boundary stone set up by your forefathers.'

The context of the scripture is one of geographical boundaries, set in place to protect farms, vineyards and the property of a particular family. There are several other references on the topic:

> 'Do not remove your neighbor's boundary...'
> (Deuteronomy 19:14)

> 'Cursed is the man who moves his neighbor's boundary stone.'
> (Deuteronomy 27:17)

> 'Men move boundary stones; they pasture flocks they have stolen.'
> (Job 24:2)

Each time the emphasis is geographical, but I want to take the principle of God's mandate for successful, co-operative living between two parties, and apply it to the young man serving the senior man in the area of doctrinal boundaries – the manner and form of teaching carried out in the church.

Who set up the boundaries?

In Joshua chapter 14 we read that Joshua, Eleazar and the tribal heads allotted land to the tribes of Israel. Zebulun had 12 towns; Benjamin 14 towns; Issachar 16 towns and so on. It was carried out '... *as the Lord commanded Moses'* (Joshua 14:5). Although it was Moses who had received the instruction, by this time he had died, so it fell to his successors to complete the task. Joshua, Eleazar, and the tribal heads carried out the actual setting of the boundaries, but the geography was down to Moses – who in turn had received his orders from the Lord.

In the same way, the senior leader is responsible to God for doctrinal boundaries – the 'geography' of what is taught and lived out in the life of the church – under orders from God. As the younger man, these boundaries should be respected and adhered to.

Scripture is not a 'closed book' when it comes to revelation. Of course I believe that God brings fresh revelation into the Church, but He does so within the boundaries of marked off doctrine. Paul reminded Timothy concerning God's Word to command it, keep it, teach it, watch it, direct it, respect it, know it, and use it. He instructed Titus to hold onto it, teach it soundly, have integrity in it, be serious about it, and deliver it with sound speech. Remember that it was God who created the doctrine, not the doctrine that created God! And He established it mainly for our benefit, not for Himself, because of our simplistic understanding, that we may know His ways better.

The senior man will probably seem, from time to time, repetitive and dry to the young man who is constantly seeking fresh revelation. This may well be true, but the young man must never seek to dislodge the doctrinal boundary stones, sacrificing them for 'instantaneous' revelation that is really no revelation at all. There is a desire in every young man to prove himself by bringing something 'new' that has never been touched on before, and that will impress the senior man. In some cases this may be possible, but only within the boundaries of doctrine.

Four keys to keeping the boundary stones in place

1. It may sound obvious, but never try to replace the foundational, proven doctrines concerning salvation

and life in the Spirit as spoken about by Jesus, with ambiguous teaching centering around humanistic, moral or ethical codes for life. 2 Peter 1:3 says,

'His divine power has given us everything we need for life and godliness through our knowledge of him.'

Don't allow anything to persuade you to begin preaching sermons that you know will 'tickle the ears' of the congregation, but actually achieve little else.

2. Spending time reading the Bible for yourself, meditating on it, and praying through it, must never be completely replaced by audio and video cassettes in a search for 'fresh' ideas. The mass media has made it very easy for us to access other people's revelation, and there is a great temptation to simply regurgitate it as if it were our own. The Holy Spirit can and will use every form of communication that the world has to offer, but never lose the ability to go to that solitary place where it is just you, your Bible and the Holy Spirit, locked away in a room.

3. The counsel of the Holy Spirit must never be replaced with the opinion of council or committee. Don't fall into the trap of preaching 'politically correct' sermons that you know will appease certain sections of the church. The first thing on your agenda must be to yield to the Holy Spirit and speak out what God has put on your heart – all with the affirmation of the senior leader.

4. The preaching of the Word, backed by personal integrity, holiness of conduct and speech, must never be replaced with either a dead, religious approach to God and His Church, or the other extreme, a gimmick orientated, light-weight presentation of the truth. Respect God's Holy Word.

The most difficult task of all is to bring fresh revelation within the given boundary stones of doctrine, because it demands we spend less time preparing on paper and more time preparing personally before God, allowing the Holy Spirit to bring you *'...knowledge of him* [Jesus]*...'* as you simply read and pray over the Scriptures. At the end of the day, which will carry more weight and authority, a superb yet coldly clinical exegesis of Scripture, or a simple truth delivered with great passion and conviction? People are seeking authenticity, not a clever presentation.

The senior man will have cultivated that discipline over many years and it needs to be worked at by the one serving. Let's conclude by taking a look at a biblical example of fresh revelation within the boundary stones of doctrine.

The day of Pentecost

The outpouring of the Holy Spirit at Pentecost was a new experience that happened in a sensational way, yet it did not become the focus of Peter's address to the crowd. If the signs and wonders were not the focal point, what was it then that caused 3000 people to be saved in a single day?

Acts 2:6 tells us that, '... *each one heard them speaking in his own language.*' There must also have been some physical manifestations accompanying, because some leveled the accusation that they had been drinking – '... *they have had too much wine*' (Acts 2:13). But whatever manifestation occurred, Peter does not mention it in his explanation. In fact many of the people in attendance were '... *bewildered ... utterly amazed ... perplexed ...*'. Instead of looking for a new or contemporary explanation, Peter looks to the established doctrinal boundaries. He begins to expound the Word of God from Joel and the Psalms (see Joel 2:28–32; Psalm 16:8–11 and Psalm 110:1). At the sound of this the multitude responded:

> '*When the people heard this they were cut to the heart and said to Peter and the other apostles, "Brothers, what shall we do?"*' (Acts 2:37)

To the man under authority I say along with Paul, as he wrote to the Colossian church,

> '*Let the Word of God dwell in you richly.*'
> (Colossians 3:16)

The senior man, again, will have cultivated over the years a knowledge of the Word that flows from him like a 'well watered garden'.

The five checks of Psalm 119

A study of the very nature of God's Word itself, before even starting on the contents, reveals an incredible depth and complexity that means you will never need to look to another source for inspiration. Psalm 119 speaks of the multi-faceted nature of the Law of God. There are five different aspects of God's Word contained in it: statutes, laws, decrees, precepts, and principles. The Psalmist prays that his way will be kept pure by adhering to them (vv. 9–16). A law is a command; a statute is an authorized law of high government; a decree is the endorsed and written law; a precept is the conduct of the law, and a principle is the application of the law expressed in a variety of ways. Who said the Scriptures are boring?!

Albert Einstein is quoted to have said at the height of his success:

'If I have seen further than any man it is because I have stood on the shoulders of great men.'

Any aspiring leader must be a student of not only the experience of the Spirit, but the way of the Spirit as prescribed in the Bible.

Chapter 6

Different Personalities but the Same Spirit

In all areas of life people are looking for someone to lead them – in politics, entertainment, business and commerce, the local church – someone that will do what they have promised to do with passion and a conviction that is contagious. An effective mentor can help a young man to develop into such a leader. He can help him to enhance his natural gifting, and will bring shape and direction to the development of his ministry. This can only happen effectively if the young man has the same spirit as the one he serves.

In Numbers 11:16–17 we read that,

> 'The Lord said to Moses, "Bring me seventy of Israel's elders who are known to you . . . and I will take the Spirit that is on you and put the Spirit on them." '

The book of Numbers could be viewed as a book of complaints to God from the people and Moses. If God had chosen 70 men for Moses, no doubt he would have complained about them, so God asked Moses to choose them instead and then He would give them the same Spirit. It was the same cloud that came upon them that had come upon Moses, under the same law, and by the same Spirit.

There is power in oneness, and a synergy that is created when people move together as 'one person'. The negative flip-side of course, is that two people diametrically opposed – i.e. not of the same spirit – will create friction instead of synergy.

The working relationship between the mentor and his protégé can become sour if, for instance, the senior man is insecure and tries to control instead of release the younger man.

The New Testament bears witness a number of times to the 'same spirit' principle. In one such instance a group that devoutly followed Judaism infiltrated the fledgling church. They did not have the same spirit as the Apostle Paul and 'infected' the converts there with their doctrine, causing devastating results. Paul was justifiably angry – *'You foolish Galatians, who has bewitched you?'* (Galatians 3:1) – because he understood the power of spiritual unity – and the opposing and destructive forces of dissension.

If your spirit is not in tune with the senior man such 'groups' can persuade you away from unity with him and poison your thinking. A snake never attacks a sparrow in a clumsy or obvious fashion, it gains eye contact and then 'bewitches' it, gradually enticing the mesmerized bird to walk towards it until the inevitable happens.

The protection of being one

A survey of five hundred people was taken to find out what were the most common reactions they had after finding out they were wrong or mistaken over a particular issue. The survey revealed that the three most common feelings by far that they experienced were the 'fear' of being punished, a sense of 'worthlessness,' and 'isolation.' Think of the times Jesus reassured His disciples of their importance in the plans of God, and how patient He was towards their lack of understanding. While they were with Him, security was their companion. But separated from Him – as they were when He was on trial before His crucifixion – these three feelings characterized them. In the same way, it is sometimes impossible to see the covering protection your mentor brings until you are separated from him.

Popular while with him

Many who serve a senior leader fail to see that, wherever he goes, they go too, and whoever he meets, they meet too – but only under his covering. All the time the young man is riding on the reputation of a better man but can fail to see the reality of it. He may accompany the senior man to large meetings and assist him in ministering to many at an altar call, but would never get such an opportunity on his own at this stage in his ministry. He may even be 'wined and dined' whilst assisting the senior man, but would not even get to McDonalds on his own merit! To anyone who is currently serving a senior man, consider the benefits of being with him before deciding to leave him. Most of all listen to the voice of the Spirit who will help to keep you in unity.

The senior man is not a monster!

In the story of Joseph's fortunes in Genesis 37:21 there is a telling phrase:

> *'When Reuben heard this, he tried to rescue him from their hands. "Let's not take his life. Don't shed any blood." '*

As the eldest son, one might assume that Reuben would have been all for killing the boy who took his place as his father's favorite, but his heart was moved and he had mercy on Joseph instead. So it is with the senior man. His desire is to see you become whole, fully equipped and trained. He is investing his life into your development. If you are not intending to leave him one day and go somewhere else, then you will likely inherit his congregation, his salary – which will probably by that time be more substantial, his popularity with the community, and the privilege of feeding the people with the Word. Like Reuben, he is actually a life saver for you, not an enemy. All these things will come to you one day, so in the meantime enjoy his security.

At times perhaps the senior man seems harsh and over-bearing to you, but the fact is shaping character in someone is not a task for the faint-hearted. Take note also of the biblical examples, God sometimes uses extreme tactics to keep His servants in line. Remember Jonah for example – the belly of a fish was perhaps not the most attractive means to an end, but it was God's way of producing 'the goods' at the end of the day. And what about Balaam's mule – have you ever felt like taking a stick to the senior man? He may be stubborn but he can rescue you from disaster!

I heard of a story that for me, really characterizes the senior man and his student. A rare bird was trapped in a thorn bush desperately trying to set itself free. An old man reached in to release it but was bitten by the bird each time he tried. Eventually the bird was set free to live a long life, but not until he had left an old man's hand bleeding. So it is with one who decides to father the next generation.

When you both start to disagree

Without a shadow of doubt we can all say that agreement, in the many activities of life, is a powerful force. Agreement can really work for us. Conversely, a lack of agreement can really work against us! In spiritual terms it was the very reason that Lucifer was cast out of heaven. God is God and no-one can dispute that. Lucifer disagreed about it and suffered the consequences of his rebellion. Since his expulsion from heaven he has roamed about the earth, masquerading in the form of many warped personalities with malicious intent against the Church and the Kingdom of God. It is no surprise that one of his greatest weapons is to cause disagreement or dissension between Christians – and how effective he is at it! Sin, in essence, is disagreement – a failure to agree with God and go His way; a deliberate choice to head in the other direction. Thankfully, the cohesive power of sin has been broken by the victory Jesus won on the cross. Identifying ourselves with Jesus' work on the cross brings us back into agreement with God.

It is disagreement, more than anything, that will build a wall between you and the senior man. The more rampant a disagreement is, the higher the wall becomes, and the harder it is to overcome. I am not talking about the times when you must 'agree to disagree' on certain topics, or the fact that you may feel isolated on occasions because the senior man knows, through his greater experience, what to do and you don't, but rather about willful dissension – an attitude that says, 'who does he think he is anyway? I'm better than he is.'

Once the devil has brought two leaders, one made and one in the making, into disagreement like that, the local church is destined to suffer eventually. This attitude also leads to all kinds of maverick behavior that would never otherwise be countenanced. Imagine for a moment that you are conducting a service at your church. You get up to minister and something happens that needs to be dealt with. You tackle it like the seven sons of Sceva (see Acts 19:13) – without success and relying on your self-confidence, rather than the gifting of God within you. Our submission to God has a direct bearing on the measure we advance in the Kingdom of God. A strong rebellion or disagreement with the senior man will invariably result in a clash either privately, or worse still, publicly. Be wise and realize that sometimes it is far better to lay aside your strongly held ideals and submit. Obedience is **always** better than sacrifice!

The importance of having the 'same spirit', or living in agreement with one another can hardly be overstated. It is an essential ingredient in an effective mentor–apprentice relationship. Once unity is at work, it will have a synergistic effect that will establish a dynamic team, and bring about great blessing for the body of believers you serve as they benefit from clear and cohesive leadership under God.

Chapter 7

'That Which I Pass on to You'

A key function in the relationship between a leader and his apprentice is that of the 'transfer' of knowledge and experience. In order for the young man to develop and grow, the senior man must seek to impart all he has learned to his protégé, so that he is built up and prepared for future leadership responsibilities. Sometimes this will happen during one to one sessions, or time spent traveling together, as the two chat and discuss various issues. But in the busy and demanding role of church leader, more often such training will take place 'organically' – i.e. the young man will learn by observation as the senior man goes about his business. Looking to the example of Christ, we see these two forms at work. Clearly it was important to Him to take His disciples away to a quiet place from time to time and impart to them 'inside knowledge' about His ways and methods. But He also advocated the 'seeing then doing' approach – His disciples would see Him in action and then try to emulate Him.

One of the most difficult aspects of this kind of training for a young man, is when the time comes for the leader to bring correction and guidance. From time to time, as the young man 'launches out' to do something, he will inevitably make mistakes. At this point the senior leader needs to spend time with him disseminating what went wrong, what could have been done differently, what approach needs to be taken next time etc., whilst offering encouragement, which should be a consistent ingredient of such conversations. Barney Coombs comments,

'When a genuine father is observing his son's mistakes, he will be careful not to be too quick to make negative comments. He knows that by accentuating the positive, he will get more of the same, and will also build up a nice amount of "credit" in the bank of approval that will help cover the "withdrawals" of correction that will be necessary at a later date.'[1]

Some find this kind of 'post mortem' easier to handle than others. Sometimes correction can be painful, especially if a significant error has been made publicly – perhaps whilst preaching to the church. But it must be viewed as an essential part of the training process by both parties. How you react to correction will dictate, to a large degree, how you develop. There are one or two specific areas I want to identify by way of example:

Personal ministry styles

Every person has their own style of ministry – the way they present teaching and preaching, the way they pray, and their general conduct when ministering. Even though we are all serving the same Lord, God's Spirit is moving through the 'filter' of our unique personality and character. What a dry and mundane world it would be if we were all 'spiritual clones'! Clearly God intended there to be such variety and color. Your senior leader will have developed his own style of ministry over the years and will be comfortable functioning in that way. The danger arises for the young man when he fails to discern the difference between things the senior man does due to personal preference, and things he does because of the anointing of the Holy Spirit – the way he lays hands on people for example, or the use of prophetic symbolism.

I have no doubt that many young men serving a senior leader will, especially at the beginning of their service, not only emulate his general style of ministry, but probably also his mannerisms, speech, character, maybe even his dress code! There is nothing essentially wrong with this 'mirror image'. In fact it shows the respect, or even awe, that the young man initially has for his senior. But clearly there will come a time when to carry on in this fashion would be unhealthy and inhibit the young man's natural growth and development. Young men need to be allowed to express their own personalities through ministry, and be nurtured, guided, corrected, encouraged, but never squashed or suppressed.

Your individual style and character separate you from the senior man. They are unique, God-given attributes that make you who you are and they should be brought out and enhanced. Of course, they may need to be refined, but not suppressed. So far, we have talked mainly from the perspective of the younger man, but what about the senior man's reaction to the emergence of his apprentice's individual style of ministry? The more confidence and success the younger man gains, the more likely it is that an increasing divergence in styles will occur. The senior man may react in one of two ways – either negatively or positively.

The first way – he frowns upon it

If you have both realized that you are in this thing together for the long haul, and the aim of your being together is for the senior man to pass the leadership over to you one day, then there could be a high expectancy on the senior man's part that you will perpetuate his style of leadership – the same style that the people have been accustomed to and that was in force as the church grew. In one sense, the leader who thinks this way has a very valid point – a sudden change of approach may bring about too great a shock to a stable congregation. It makes sense though, in any transfer of leadership, for there to be a clear and well-defined, well-timed transition between the leader retiring and his apprentice assuming his mantle, with the resulting change in style. There is much security to be found in 'keeping things the way they are', though more often than not, such 'security' is just an excuse for avoiding the challenge of change.

When I refer to 'change' in this context, I do not mean anything except the change of individual style. For instance, the senior man may speak for a set time, you may not. He may be systematic in his preaching and teaching, while you may be more inspirational and spontaneous. He may not use much body language, while you may flap around like a chicken in order to make your point! He may speak slowly, whereas you may speak quickly as if commentating a horse race! The list of subtle differences in style could go on and on. The danger is that the senior man could start to think that you have not listened to a word he has said over the years about how to deliver a sermon, and are completely ignoring his advice, but in it all you are still under his ministry serving him, so keep a right spirit about you.

The second way – he loves you for it

Dr Martin Lloyd Jones has been quoted as saying, 'I would not cross the road to hear myself preach.' He obviously held lightly onto his ministry. However, if a leader is a solitary man, who has kept to the same style all his ministerial life, the chances are that he will be quietly, proud of who he is and what he stands for. To work with such a man is not an easy task. If however, he has managed to change and adapt his style as the need arose over the years, then he will probably delight to see a further development of himself in you. Often it depends on how the senior man himself came to the place where he is now. Did he serve another man in his younger days? Or has he always been a trail-blazer – going it alone?

In my own experience, when I presented various projects that I felt would be good for the church to the senior leader I served, the reply would often be a positive one. If it was an additional church meeting or event he would encourage me in it, without giving me the expectation that he would always attend it. As a young man, never feel a sense of discouragement if the senior man does not show up himself at your events. Instead of feeling disappointed, viewing his absence as a lack of interest or enthusiasm, rather take full advantage of the opportunity he has given you to relax without being observed – he will still want to know what happened afterwards!

Different philosophical approaches

Have you ever wondered why the service restaurants on motorways have the desserts lined up before the savory food?

It doesn't make sense to present a dessert before a main course. Or does it? It wasn't always done that way, but marketing executives discovered that a dessert can be presented in a way that whets the appetite of the consumer and creates a greater chance of them actually buying it. The senior man may have always had a 'meat and potatoes' ministry. Perhaps you have a more colorful and attractive ministry, and you would like to see the desserts being offered first! It may just be that the fresh approach you will bring inspires the church and spurs it on to greater things. Basic truths that all of us take for granted can often be brought suddenly to life by injecting some stimulating new methods of presentation. It has been estimated that the technology of the world doubles every 1.7 years, the net result of which is many more and exciting ways in which to present information. It may just be that you are the change that the local church is waiting for. They have been hearing the same word for years, but suddenly it takes on a new and dynamic dimension as that same word is presented with copious variety.

Both you and your senior leader will have a philosophy of life that is largely influenced by your personality, your experience and your training. They all combine to make up your own personal perspective on life. Inevitably this 'psyche' has an effect of how you understand the Scriptures and how they are practically applied to your life and ministry. It is unavoidable – a part of our human frailty and vulnerability. Once we learn a certain way of doing something, if it works for us, we are reluctant to depart from it. In Jeremiah chapter 31 we read of the New Covenant that God intends to establish. It is described as not being like the Old Covenant – written on stone tablets – but rather one that is written on the hearts and minds of God's people, and one that will distinguish the people of God in relation to Him. The young student may think that the senior man still reads from the stone tablets every morning over breakfast to his enduring wife! But this is little more than a matter of 'mindset' in one or both of the parties. It is worth remembering that the senior man's methods of ministry, however tired they may seem to you, work for him – and they also 'work'! He wouldn't be successful if they didn't.

How you react in thought, as well as deed

An important key to a successful working relationship is the ability to separate in your mind the wisdom and anointing of the senior man from his working practices – the ways of doing things that you may feel are hackneyed and worn out. 1 Peter 1:13 says, *'Gird up the loins of your mind.'* The expression is a common one. It was the phrase used to describe the prophet Elijah as he tucked his cloak in his belt, enabling him to run fast ahead of the king's chariot (1 Kings 18:48). The idea conveyed by Peter is one of preparing for action, being on guard and alert – ready to deal ruthlessly with any stray thought.

This is important, because a young man can be destroyed by his own thinking if he does not take hold of every thought regarding the senior man that might wander unchallenged through his mind. An increasing lack of respect towards him can steadily build as one critical thought after another goes unchecked.

The power of impartation

We have focused on some of the 'danger areas' in the relationship between senior leader and apprentice, in order to be in a position to identify potential problems and deal with them before they develop, but the greatest positive aspect is the process of impartation that takes place as the mentor seeks to educate his protégé. An experienced man, who has proven the faithfulness of God over many years and seen Him at work time and again, can stir up faith in his apprentice and inspire him to go on to do greater things for God. I believe that a young man in this position will develop more quickly and grow with a healthier perspective of ministry than someone who is trying to be a trail-blazer – working through problems on his own and having to learn from his own mistakes. I am not saying it cannot be done! It is simply that I view the God of the Bible as a generational God, who is concerned with one generation educating the next with regard to His ways, and that the Bible also provides us with many examples of effective mentoring.

Character is vital

> 'For therein is the righteousness of God revealed from faith to
> faith as it is written, "The just shall live by faith." '
>
> (Romans 1:17 KJV)

I believe this verse refers not to the saving grace of God believed by faith (Ephesians 2:8), or the gift of faith (1 Corinthians 12:9), but the constant developing of your spirit in tune with the Holy Spirit as it remains teachable. Many will be saved through faith in Jesus Christ, and many will desire to operate in the gift of faith, but fewer may develop to maturity in the fruit of the Spirit. It is all to do with 'character'. The development of character – having Christ formed in you – is a tough, though essential business. God will use a variety of people, circumstances and situations to get the job done.

The senior man will probably put you through trying times. Although not always pleasant, it will invariably develop a character and accompanying faith in you that will eventually reveal an edge to your prayer life that would otherwise not have been there. Enduring the difficulties of life and proving God's faithfulness through them builds **character** and **faith** – they go hand in hand.

We all suffer from a measure of doubt from time to time, but character and faith must be developed in you by the Holy Spirit, under the senior man. The Spirit of God does not have an ounce of unbelief in Him. If young men are to lead a church then the people have to know that your word is your bond. That you are not presenting a vision to them because of what you 'feel', but because of what you 'know' in the Spirit. In the opening chapter of Jeremiah the Lord asks him twice *'What do you see?'* God Himself does not need an answer to this question, but is seeking to give Jeremiah the ability to see His divine purpose by faith. In the same respect Jesus asked the blind man at Bethsaida, *'What do you see?'* He responded, *'I see men as trees.'* Again Jesus prayed, wanting the man himself to believe by faith.

Many leaders, responsible for training young men coming into ministry, must have struggled with the dilemma:

'What's more important, to train him to preach skill-fully, or to teach him to turn the other cheek? Do I focus on building a strong leadership style, or concen-trate on encouraging him to team-build?'

Believe me when I say that the senior man has a difficult task in preparing you. He has no easy options. He can't afford to concentrate too much on developing any one aspect to the detriment of another. What good is a man who is respected, yet preaches a shallow and meaningless message? Equally, what good is a man who preaches skillfully, but whose life and conduct are a sham?

The moral of this message is this: **trust**. You have to believe that God has your best interests at heart – because He has! He will use your leader and allow him to correct you in many areas. For your own sanity however, you must never interpret a critical comment directed at one area as an attack on the whole. Even though you may have delivered a tremendous message and blessed the congregation, the senior man may have to correct you on your conduct with them afterwards. The mature young man will separate the two and not feel 'got at'.

Your mentor desires to pass on to you all he can. He will also realize that some things may be hard for you to take, but still very necessary for your development. In all of this it is helpful to realize that, first of all the Lord, your Father, and secondly your senior leader, have your best interests at heart. Gaining a little more humility through serving and learning will do you no harm at all, so humble yourself and keep your thoughts upon God, who is about the business of making you a leader of distinction.

Reference

1. Coombs, Barney. *Apostles Today, Christ's Love-gift to the Church*, 1996, Sovereign World.

Chapter 8

What About My Wife?

Joseph Conrad said:

> 'Being a woman is a difficult trade, since it consists principally of dealing with men.'

I believe God gave me a wife that He had spent twenty-one years lovingly developing especially to handle me! She has been, and is, a wonderful support to me and is always the most 'truthful' barometer of my ministry and moods. I cannot think of any other woman that could live with me and put up with the things I do! I believe, like Adam, that God foreknew exactly what type of woman I needed.

As I grew up I had three opportunities to develop a lasting relationship. Like most young men these came through dating. Looking back, one of these girls has now turned away from God, and another has sadly died of a brain tumor. The third, I am glad to say, 'stole my heart' and became a loving wife, and later on a mother to Daniel and Zachery, our two sons.

The unique relationship between a man and his wife provides yet another area of challenge to the young man serving under a senior minister. Leading a church can be incredibly time-consuming, exhausting and frustrating, as well as a privilege, a joy and an honor! It can also involve much traveling and time spent away from home if the senior leader has a well-developed itinerant ministry, and even without that dimension, there will be many and various intrusions into your personal life. Of course you are there to serve the Body of Christ by leading, and that means being accessible and available to help people with their problems, but you must also protect and nurture your personal relationships too.

It is vital for a young man to retain the utmost integrity in his relationship with his wife. A stable home life will provide a solid base for ministry and so make you all the more effective. You cannot, however, pour all your time and effort into trying to minister effectively, only giving your wife (and children if you have any) the dregs of your time, and expect it all to work out OK in the end! It will not happen that way. There have been too many young men who, whilst they could not be faulted for their dedication and commitment to the Gospel, have sadly neglected their spouses and arrived home one day from a trip to find them gone – unable to cope with the isolation any longer. What is the result of this? The young man's ministry is de-railed and ceases to function as it once did. How much better it would have been to have prioritized things differently and still have a successful ministry today, instead of ending up burnt out and divorced.

I would like to present a check list for you to stimulate your thinking in this area, built from my own experiences of marriage. These are questions you should ask yourself as you prepare to enter the ministry. Firstly to the wives:

1. Can you be content to stay at home with the children whilst your husband is away ministering to others?

2. Can you watch your husband love and care for others in the church as well as you?

3. Can you watch your husband sometimes being stabbed in the back by those he loves?

Secondly, to the husbands:

1. Can you give quality time with your wife priority over the church?

2. Can you be disciplined enough not to take your stress out on her?

3. Can you protect her from comments that are made about her?

These are all real issues and you should be realistic about your expectations of what 'being in ministry' actually involves. Usually, pre-marital courses, where available, will raise issues of compatibility in areas such as money and economics, family and friends, hobbies, sex, and so on. But nobody can prepare you for the kind of 'marriage under stress' you may live out as a pastor and pastor's wife. Anyone already serving under a senior man who wants to get married should first think about some of the issues here and talk them through with his fiancée. Serving a senior man is hard enough, but to be married to a someone serving that man is even more demanding.

Your wife's attitude tends to become like yours

Every woman wants to be proud of her husband, and it is quite likely that your wife, from time to time, will perceive that you are being treated like an 'office boy' or being made to be a 'yes man' to the senior minister. Your wife may see the practical implications before the spiritual implications and questions them. It is possible for a two-fold problem to emerge here: firstly, you may be having a testing time because the 'servant' aspect of your role is at the fore and you are not enjoying it very much. Maybe the senior man is asking you to do things that are frustrating you and causing you stress. Secondly, your wife has identified this and is unhappy about the way you are being treated, knowing that 'you deserve better'! This is a critical time in which integrity must be maintained.

It is so easy to arrive home and spend a great deal of time airing your grievances, but this does nothing but add fuel to the fire that is already simmering in your wife! If your conversation about the senior man is critical and demeaning in the home, then a wedge will be driven between the love you have for your wife and the loyalty you have for the one you serve. Not only that, but you will 'reproduce' that feeling in your wife too. Incredible arguments and 'domestic situations' may erupt over trivial issues that would have been brushed aside under normal circumstances. Because of your intimate involvement, it is not just your emotions but your heart that is torn.

It is crucial to get the balance right in these relationships. Your wife must see that her husband possesses a strength and determination to put her first, before the senior man, and before the local church. This is not just 'right' it is absolutely biblical. She must also see that, even when you are going through a hard time, you maintain a godly perspective on it, and keep your respect for the senior leader. When you start to do that, she will have the same respect for the senior man as you do – and her attitude will again become like yours.

On the wrong side of the desk

Sometimes, the senior man will not be aware of the intense emotions that may be exploding between you and your wife, or at least, he may not be at first! At these times, if you have a solid and open relationship with him, you should make an opportunity to explain that your relationship with him is driving a wedge between you and your wife. Although he is not guilty of any division himself, but simply ignorant of the situation, and if he can see that you are placing the 'wife of your youth' before him, he should, and will, have an admiration for your determination to build on a sure foundation. A wise senior man will do something to help this situation, maybe through his wife to your wife. Never forget that the senior man and his wife were a young married couple themselves, and the reason you can learn so much from him is that he has already been where you are!

Entering the forbidden zone

I mentioned briefly in Chapter 4, two potential areas of conflict in the relationship between the young man and senior leader: his wife and his children. They are all members of the church in which you are a minister, and you have a delegated authority and responsibility for their spiritual welfare, just like any other church member – or do you?!

Dealing with these two areas is like entering 'the Forbidden Zone'. They are rarely, if ever, taught about or discussed –

probably least of all by the senior man! They are difficult to deal with at the best of times and it is often hard to know what action to take:

1. The senior man can bring you correction for your edification and encouragement. But what if his wife starts doing it too? Does she have the same rights of access to your life as the senior man does?

2. His children will be familiar, or even 'over' familiar with you, after all, you are often in their house with their father, taking up time that he should be spending with them. On top of that, what if his wife becomes a little jealous of the time he spends with you instead of his children?

You can quickly see why these two areas are located in 'the Forbidden Zone'. For these kind of issues, no simple pat answers exist, and I would be doing you a disservice be pretending there are easy solutions, or by writing some all-encompassing platitude. What I can tell you is that you are going to have to develop relationships on many levels with the senior man and his family and learn to juggle them accordingly. It may even be, though this is not the ideal, that these relationships are far removed from the ones you have with the rest of the congregation. Perhaps you are surprised that I am suggesting such anomalies should be allowed to exist. I'm not, but we are dealing with reality here – and things like this occur in real life! As always, be prepared and armed with humility and the grace of God.

Precious vows before each other and God

Before we were married, Renee and I had an understanding between us that God had called me to serve Him within the Body of Christ, and that she, as my future wife, had been called to serve with me in that capacity. After careful consideration and prayer, we decided to 'make public' the commitment we had already made to each other in engage-ment, and get married. We were very aware of the fact that our covenant was being made, not only before our respective family members and friends, but before all of heaven, and so we searched the Word of God to make some personal and meaningful additions to the traditional vows that would underline the seriousness of our intent. This was the promise my wife made to me at 11:00 am on 10 July 1993, our wedding day:

> *'Where you go I will go, and where you stay I will stay. Your people will be my people and your God my God. Where you die I will die, and there I will be buried. May the Lord deal with me, be it ever so severely, if anything but death separates you from me.'* (Ruth 1:16–17)

My vow to her in addition to the traditional promises was:

> *'You have stolen my heart, my sister, my bride; you have stolen my heart.'* (Song of Songs 4:9)

Church life is busy, but always remember, your personal walk with God must come first, and then your relationship with your wife and children.

Setting the pattern

If the relationship a young man has with the senior man is not prioritized in the context of his marriage the pattern for his own children will also be sealed. Children learn to imitate what you do. The way you treat others, the way you behave, speak, and conduct yourself, all contribute to the lesson of life that your children will be constantly absorbing. Whilst ministering overseas I picked up a poem, whose author is unknown, that sums up what it is to have a right spirit about you as a father, being mindful of the watchful eyes of your children:

> 'A careful man I want to be,
> A little fellow follows me.
> I do not dare to go astray,
> For fear he'll go the self same way.
> I cannot escape his eyes,
> Whatever he sees me do he tries,

Like me, he says he going to be,
The little chap who follows me.
He thinks that I am good and fine,
Believes in every word of mine,
The base in me he must not see,
The little chap who follows me.
I must remember as I go,
Through summer's sun and winter's snow,
I am building for the years to be,
That little chap who follows me.'

A highly favored wife?

Mary, the mother of Jesus, was 'highly favored' by God. She was a pure woman, a virgin, and a godly woman who feared the Lord. A pure and God-fearing wife is the greatest asset any man could ever have, especially one who desires to accomplish great things in God's kingdom. In Luke 1:28, as well as being identified as 'highly favored' the angel of the Lord also says to Mary that, '...*the Lord is with you...*' There is no higher accolade than to hear people say of your wife that 'the Lord is with her.' There is something about the countenance of a woman who walks with God that is radiant. I am not speaking of natural features or attractiveness, but the glory of God upon her. Have you ever considered that Mary made a major biological contribution to the face of Jesus? In His face there was something that attracted everyone from the children of Palestine to the Pharisee called Nicodemus. The Scriptures go on to say that He grew in wisdom and stature before men and God. As well as the working of the Holy Spirit in Him, the ones who were responsible for Him as a child – His earthly parents, Mary and Joseph – must also have played a major role in the equation.

A 'highly favored' wife will provide the most solid base for successful ministry and don't forget that she will take her lead from you in terms of attitude towards the senior man – if you are critical of him in front of her, she will adopt your ways. Like Hannah who sang, Sarah who laughed, and Mary who rejoiced, your wife will be both influential upon you, and influenced by your attitudes, so make sure you protect her.

Chapter 9

Your Salary and His

Most expressions of the church will have guidelines as to the recommended minimum pay for a minister. Most of these would also agree that the senior minister be paid at least 25% more than any other salaried member of staff. In the case of someone serving the senior man, it will most likely appear that your salary is in no way commensurate to the amount of effort being put in. However, I have proven, in the five years I served under a senior man, that the rewards for having right priorities far exceed any recommendation made by a governing body or central office. To put this into perspective let me share with you some of the experiences of those five years in relation to money.

I moved away from Nottingham, the place of my home church, to work under a senior man indefinitely for £100 sterling a week in December 1990, after earning a good salary in secular employment. After two months even the £100 per week stopped due to lack of funds and no further income was forthcoming. I had to subsidize my income while the senior man continued to receive his income and maintain the same standard of living. I eventually sold the house I owned in Nottingham for less than I purchased it for, leaving me with no equity and forcing me to live in a single-room apartment. Over the next two years I continued to serve the senior man and took any opportunity that came my way work-wise to support myself. For the remaining three years, I still received no income due to the financial situation of the church. Some expenses were paid however, and in the last year, a monthly offering was taken that amounted to, on average, £120 per month. During all this time I had no car of my own to get around in or to take my future wife out on a date, except for the final year when I acquired a seventeen-year-old Austin Maxi! The times I went to bed torn between the call of God on my life and a desire to give it all up and return to 'comfortable' secular work were far more than I care to remember. I don't recount these events to point the finger and say, 'How badly they treated me!' God used these events to chisel and shape my character for future use. Looking back, although I didn't get a salary, the senior man did many other things for me that were above and beyond the call of duty. God taught me things about money during that time that have remained with me ever since, and the most important thing of all that He taught me was to throw myself wholeheartedly into full dependence upon Him as the source of all my needs.

Four principles

1. Money can make you and your home look good but, it can never replace the anointing.

2. Money, like manure, is only effective when it is spread about!

3. Money has made more men covetous than covetousness has made men rich.

4. A man who has a little will show much appreciation for what is given to him, but a rich man rarely says thank you.

Thankfully, the days when the motto of the church was 'keep him poor to keep him humble' are pretty much over. A man has to live, and unless God has called him specifically to a unique 'walk of faith', he cannot be expected to do his job whilst living on thin air, just because he is a Christian. So, notwithstanding exceptional circumstances, a young man should be paid a realistic wage to meet his reasonable needs. I qualify that statement by saying 'reasonable needs' because we must always maintain a sensible balance. A young man may need a car to transport him and his family around, but he does not 'need' a Jaguar XJS in order to accomplish this!

We must not fall prey to a 'poverty mindset' with regard to money however. Our God is eminently capable of supplying our every need. There will be times when God just wants to bless you beyond all your expectations, simply because He is a lavish and joyful Giver and a generous Father. All that is needed for you to fulfil the purposes of God's plans for you have already been accounted for in God's economy – both spiritual resources in Christ, and material resources on earth. These great truths expressed throughout Scripture come into operation as we grasp hold of them, understand them in our heart, and finally, put them to the test by practising them.

Writing to the scattered Christians in Asia Minor, the Apostle Peter says,

> '*His divine power has given us everything we need for* **life** *and godliness through our knowledge of him . . . '*
>
> (2 Peter 1:3)

God already has all the resources you need for life at hand, even if you don't see them yet.

Within these pages I am not suggesting that every senior man is perfect or that the younger men serving are the ideal successors. My intention is to set forth an outline of the relationship, how it works, the challenges, pitfalls, and what to expect in such a partnership. Sometimes there are unbalanced relationships, particularly when it comes to money. It may be that you feel you are not being treated fairly, but rather than reacting negatively, keep your integrity before the Lord and others. If you have truly entrusted your life and ministry into God's hands, then let Him be the judge of whether you are being treated justly or not. So far, God has given me the privilege of ministering on three continents. I have seen sights and experienced things that I never would have, had I not been serving God. God has blessed me and my family – He is no man's debtor!

1 Peter 2:23–24 says,

> *...instead, he entrusted himself to him who judges justly.*
> *He himself bore our sins in his body...'*

In the context of this passage Peter is referring to a description of Jesus from Isaiah 53 as his format for speaking to Christian Jews scattered throughout Asia Minor. In that Old Testament chapter there are three specific phrases that describe what Jesus did for us. They will help any young man who feels he is being dealt with unjustly.

1. *'Surely he has borne our grief...'* (Isaiah 53:4).

2. *'...he will bear their iniquities...'* (Isaiah 53:11).

3. *'...for he bore the sin of many...'* (Isaiah 53:12).

We have a picture of Jesus walking to the cross with all the sin of this world – none of it His – bearing all our grief (our condition) and iniquity (the consequence of that condition) like a heavy weight upon His back. Then as they crucified Him, He lifted it all up to God. Peter points out the fact that Jesus did not fight or justify Himself, but committed Himself to that which He was born for and let God justify Him. Many prophetic statements throughout Scripture speak of the reward that awaited Jesus. If every young man who is treated in an unjust way has the stomach and strength to follow the example of Jesus, then the end product will be a an incredibly focused and strong leadership based on refined and purified character, certain of God's call and anointing and unaffected by a lack of integrity in others. That is what you must always aim for, so don't allow yourself to be derailed by money or any other material distraction.

Chapter 10

When it's Time to Leave

There inevitably comes a time in the relationship between senior leader and apprentice where a natural state divergence occurs. Management theories focusing on leadership in the context of team-building tell us that the natural progression in such relationships consists of three stages:

1. **dependence** – where team-members are totally dependent on their leader;

2. **independence** – where team-members gain in confidence and begin to operate in their own areas; and

3. **interdependence** – the theoretical ideal, where each person is mutually dependent on the other.

I would like to turn this model around, and suggest that the ideal to aim for is independence. I'll explain why:

At first there is almost complete **dependence**, as the younger man relies on his mentor to guide him and influence his thinking whilst he is being trained. If the senior man is successfully imparting his wisdom and skills to the young man, then this will inevitably lead to a state of **interdependence** – both should be released to function in their differing but complementary gifts, so as to become a powerful team. In a situation where team ministry is the norm, this is obviously the ideal to aim for. But what if the younger man will one day be assuming full responsibility for the leadership of the church whilst his mentor steps down, or what if the young man is 'posted' by his denomination to lead another church in a different city? That young man will need to be able to function autonomously without relying on the continual support of his former leader. He should have been trained to function independently, so that he will have the confidence to leave his mentor's covering and strike out on his own, and not least because he will eventually need to nurture a successor himself.

Only you can determine which of these two models is right for you. Has God called you to be a leader in your own right, or to serve in a supporting role? As time goes on the right option for you will become apparent. This discovery can only be made through the experience of being on your own and having a chance to lead. 'Being on your own' in this context, means being allowed to function in the leadership role and test your abilities under the authority and guidance of the senior man. I am not encouraging 'mavericks' and 'lone rangers' who wander around various churches with an 'individual' ministry that is not connected to any local body.

Some will have the ability to take the helm of a church and be the responsible man over it all; others, whilst extremely gifted, will not. If the senior man trusts you with his flock then he will probably leave you in charge while he ministers in other places or takes a holiday. It is at this time that any young man must take full advantage of sitting in the driving seat, without abusing his position of privilege and knowing full well that he will have to 'move over' in a short while. While the senior man is present you will inevitably feel protected, but when he has gone momentarily, anything could happen! What if a drunk walks into the service and starts shouting while you are giving thanks for the bread and wine? What if, at the close of your message, no-one comes forward? Or what if everyone comes forward! What are you going to do? Of course, if it is a biblically structured church there will be a team to help, but that is all they will do – help! – **you** are in charge.

The acid test

One of the key tests for knowing that it is time for you to leave the senior man and assume responsibility for a church yourself is the confirmation of the Holy Spirit speaking to you. This could happen in a variety of ways:

- the Holy Spirit speaking personally to your spirit;
- God speaking to you through passages of Scripture;
- prophetic confirmation through the ministry of others.

The ideal would be a combination of all three. Leaders do not just **assume** their positions, they are **recognized** by the people. In Acts 20:22 Paul says,

> *'And now, compelled by the Spirit, I am going to Jerusalem not knowing what will happen to me there.'* (Acts 20:22)

In the same way, the younger man will know when his 'time is up' with the senior man as the Spirit compels him to move on, maybe uncertain as to exactly what will happen next.

The key for the young man here is to be vigilant for the voice of the Holy Spirit, giving him the direction concerning where he is to go and what he is to do. The church at Ephesus where Paul was when the Spirit called him away did not want him to leave. Neither did Paul (in his own flesh) particularly want to leave – *'After we had torn ourselves away from them . . .'* (Acts 21:1). But it was time, in God's purpose, to move on. Paul could have settled where he was in any number of churches, taken a good salary and been looked after, but he had learned to obey the compelling of the Spirit. He headed towards Jerusalem, unaware at this stage that he had only two years left to live before his martyrdom. He did not know that he would have an opportunity to preach to Felix, Festus, Aggripa, or the Imperial household. He did not know that Rome itself would suffer disaster under the leadership of Nero, after Paul himself had preached there. Totally unaware of these future events he simply obeyed the urging of the Holy Spirit to go.

In a game of chess it only takes one piece to win the game, but all sixteen pieces have to contribute to the final move. Some pieces will have been taken and lost, others made redundant and rendered non-essential to the winning move of the final stages. So it is with the young man about to make his move. Many people will have bought him to this place and contributed to his being there. Some will have made a lasting impression, some a momentary contribution, but all have helped him to hear and obey the Spirit's voice. It is important then, for the young man to hear God's voice accurately, but also to heed the advice of those close to him who can generally view his situation far more objectively, and will have spoken into his life on a number of occasions previously.

The solitary place

As Paul continued his journey, landing at Tyre, he met some more 'disciples' who urged him not to continue into Jerusalem. Acts 21:4 records, *'Through the Spirit they urged Paul not to go to Jerusalem...'* The Holy Spirit can of course, reveal the same thing to the senior man as to the younger man who serves him, but there can be two different reactions. Paul heard the call of God to Jerusalem and it excited him, but others who heard it also, reacted with fear.

The same thing happened to the twelve spies sent out to survey the land of Canaan – two got excited (Joshua and Caleb), but ten got scared. Again, we find the similar reactions in Elijah and Elisha. Elisha asked Elijah for a double portion of the Spirit that was upon his life. Elijah's response was, *'You ask a difficult thing...'* (2 Kings 2:9–10).

At times such as these there can be a conflict of 'rank' between the younger and older man. The younger man is looking mostly to the future and is less interested in the present, whereas the older man has a more realistic grasp of the present and may use his experience and knowledge to deter the younger man. I believe, with all integrity, that the greatest battle is often taking place within the senior man, not the younger man. He knows exactly what his student will face and all the heartache that accompanies it, but cannot put that into words that will effectively penetrate the heart of this excited young man. Paul was **compelled** but the people were **urged**. 'Urged' means 'forcefully encouraged to do something'; 'compelled' carries the sense of 'being driven or made to do something', or at the very least inexorably drawn into it. The senior man may urge you to stay, but he knows in his heart that all his urging will not alter the compulsion being impressed upon you.

It is essential to leave with blessing

Throughout Scripture we read of blessings being given by the dying to the living, or from one man to his successor. The ability for a man to pass blessing on to another as they are released into their own ministry is an essential part of moving on. The conclusion to Paul's episode before he left for Jerusalem was a blessed one.

> *'All the disciples and their wives and children accompanied us out of the city, and there on the beach we knelt to pray.'*
> (Acts 21:5b)

> *'...the Lord's will be done.'* (Acts 21:14b)

In Paul's case a man called Agabus came to confirm what was already in his heart. Agabus was a prophet mentioned only twice in the New Testament church, but nonetheless he played his part in the big picture. He was a man with no sentimental feelings towards Paul, unlike the people around him. The senior man will have feelings about the young man that influence his attitudes towards him and consequently the action he will take. A prophet from 'outside' will not be influenced by these deep personal feelings for one about to 'move out'. If he has served and learned from the senior man over the years, the young man will be able to discern the voice of the 'prophet'. What Agabus said did not create a conflict for Paul, it simply agreed with his spirit.

The need for wise counsel

I sound a note of caution for all young men who feel God is speaking to them about moving on: choose your advisers (or the sources you allow to exert influence upon you) very carefully. Any 'prophetic' word you take on board must be from a trusted source. Do not allow yourself to be swayed by mere 'opinion' or by the feelings of the 'vocal minority' that is ever-present in any church. Ultimately, such opinions will lead you nowhere and you will be trampled upon. My own wife was once told by a lady outside our church that she would not bear children for many years, but God would eventually open her womb to produce three children. Since then we have lost touch with that lady, but if she were still around I would like to know what she would make of our son, Daniel, who arrived just three years into our marriage!

We do not have any pets in our house by choice, although as time goes by, our children may want them. When I go into a home that has a dog or cat I instantly detect it, because they give off a distinct aroma. It is not necessarily a bad smell, but a detectable one. If I were to ask the owners of that house if they could smell anything, the chances of them saying 'yes' would be remote. The reason for this is that they constantly live 'in' the aroma of their pets, and I don't. It is not out of the question, therefore, to listen to a man who does not know you intimately, but can look at what God is saying to you with a greater sense of objectivity and realism. He is not constantly surrounded by the aroma – but you are. That is not to say the young man should not listen to those closest to him, who love him and have a vested interest in his future, but always check that the **compelling** is coming from the Holy Spirit.

Chapter 11

Are You Strong Enough?

Although the relationship between an apprentice and his mentor is a highly beneficial and rewarding one, it must ultimately come to an end if its true purpose is to be achieved – that of releasing the young man to stand on his own two feet and become a leader in his own right, and of course, a mentor and role model to other young men. It is intended to be a generational process, so for the young man to remain indefinitely with the senior man is self-defeating. This does not mean however, that all ties to the senior man must be severed. He will always be a mentor, but now his role changes to one of objective observer and adviser, rather than 'hands-on' trainer and facilitator.

When you do finally part company with your senior leader, it is always good practice and protocol to maintain a healthy relationship with him, because there will be more times than you imagine when you will need to go back to him for advice. However, at the initial time of your separation, you will need to display a great deal of personal discipline and strength. You can no longer comfort yourself with the thought that it is your senior leader who is ultimately responsible for actions taken and decisions made – now this privilege is yours! I would like to explore the experiences of five biblical characters, drawing parallels from their lives to the young man who has just struck out on his own. They are Daniel, Gideon, Elisha, Joseph and John the Baptist.

Daniel and compromise

We are told that Daniel was of noble birth, but was carried away to Babylon as a boy. He excelled in many different areas because he proved himself strong and always kept his focus, even though he was out of his familiar surroundings. He said 'no' to food sacrificed to idols. He said 'no' to the worship of pagan idols. Through his hardships he learned greater skills for leadership. He did not compromise on the values he had learned from his home country. Similarly, the young man must keep his focus, remind himself of the values he has learnt, and refuse to compromise by taking the line of least resistance. The lessons that he so carefully observed when alongside his former teacher, should be so ingrained that they are like natural instincts. A good conscience is as precious as gold, so never compromise when you know that something is wrong, and always face up to issue, even when it hurts.

Gideon and glory

During Gideon's lifetime, Israel was in a state of judgement and under attack from the Midianites. He was called to a place of leadership, but was notable due to the fact that he never sought glory for himself. He demonstrated his strength by destroying all the idolatry in Israel. He trusted God by taking 300 men (when he could have opted for the 'safety in numbers' of many more) and destroyed the enemy. The people then turned to him and wanted him to be king. He demonstrated his awareness of God's purpose for his life by refusing the glory of kingship. Never be tempted away from what God has told you to do by the attraction of temporary glory. Go for long-term significance rather than short-term success. Don't try to bless if God has told you to build. In other words, don't allow all your time to be taken up by traveling the country speaking at conferences when God has instructed you to spend your time building up the local church. For some that will be right, but you must only do what God has told you to do. Gideon is also for us a case-study in humility. Even in small matters we must resist the temptation to 'snatch' the glory that rightfully belongs to God. The Lord ably demonstrated to Gideon that it was He, and He alone, that was responsible for their victory by forcing Gideon to go into battle with a ridiculously small number of troops. It would have been totally inappropriate then for Gideon to seize the opportunity to become king – as if he were the one whose brilliant strategy had won the day.

Elisha and money

As the well known story goes, Naaman, the commander of King Aram's army, had leprosy and sought after the ministry of Elisha. He was healed after being obedient to the prophet's bidding. Having been healed, Naaman then offered Elisha 750 lbs of silver, 150 lbs of gold, and ten sets of fine clothing. Although there is nothing wrong with receiving the wealth of the world *per se*, in this case Elisha saw that it was not right and refused it – the grace of God cannot be purchased. He demonstrated his strength by saying no to great wealth as a reward for what was after all, God's power, not his own. He was imitating that which his mentor, Elijah, had taught him, if not by word, by example. You must exercise wisdom with the money that God allows to pass through your hands. Again, the golden rule is that you must fall back on the values you have learned. Don't suddenly start living extravagantly because you are now in the position of 'senior minister' and have a greater income than before. Remember the 'lean' times when **anything** you received was a bonus! You may soon have younger men serving under you, and you will have an opportunity to teach, train and show them kindness in the same way your mentor did to you.

Joseph and sex

As a young man Joseph was perhaps unwise in telling his brothers the dreams God gave him. The trouble was, he was so 'full' of his destiny that it was bursting out of him. However, through the various challenges of his life, he grew in wisdom. At one such juncture, the wife of his master offered him adulterous sex. To his own temporary detriment he said 'no' demonstrating an ability to remain strong where many would have fallen. He was able to draw upon the lessons he had learned on his personal journey. Money, sex and power are cited as the three biggest traps of ministry. People are naturally attracted to those 'in power' and the potent mix of emotions that this attraction can create can be translated in all sorts of wrong and harmful ways. One of the greatest assets you have is your integrity. Once you lose it, it can be very difficult to regain. Whilst I could write an entire chapter on safeguards for practical ministry, that is not our purpose here. Let me make a blanket statement by saying that the best form of defense, in this case, is offense. Don't allow yourself to be put in a vulnerable position. Be alert to the possibility of 'attraction' between you and a church member and work to put the necessary safeguards in place. Protect the precious anointing God has given you. (For excellent practical guidelines on this subject, I recommend reading *A Guide to Practical Pastoring* by Barney Coombs, Sovereign World.)

John the Baptist and status

John, the last prophet before Jesus, had the prestige of a modern day preacher and attracted a great deal of public curiosity. He influenced everyone from the Gentiles to the rulers of Jerusalem. But there came a day when he recognized the *'Lamb of God who takes away the sin of the world.'* From that day on he knew that the emphasis was not going to be on his ministry, but on that of Jesus the Messiah – the very subject he had centered his own ministry on. He showed his strength by declaring that he was to decrease whilst Christ would increase. He said 'no' to personal prestige in preference to the Kingdom. If money, sex and power are the major 'corrupters' of a man, power (or status) is the greatest of them. Power corrupts and absolute power corrupts absolutely, it has been said. As a young man assuming your first senior role, it is right that you should desire to gain the respect and trust of your congregation, but never seek power or prestige. Power can often be gained by those with the most charisma, but it is superficial and will ultimately be found to be lacking in substance. You may enjoy power and prestige while they last, but sooner or later someone with more charisma will come along and you will be left in a vacuum. From the very beginning of your ministry, make a decision to expose any personal ambitions for power – however deeply buried under the surface of your character – and allow God to endow you with humility. Surrendering to God and refusing to play the 'power game' is a mark of greatness. In the same way that John recognized that he was not 'the one', you must also be aware of your own strengths and weaknesses. When you see someone who is more gifted than you in a particular area, step aside and allow them to function under your authority. It would have been futile for John to do anything other than decrease in deference to Jesus, and you must do the same when appropriate.

So, if all five examples are applied to the character and ministry of a man, he will be strong when it comes to compromise, glory, money, sex, and power. It is easy to see in retrospect, how important it is to learn the relevant lessons whilst under the care of your mentor. Whilst under his authority you are in a protected and safe environment, and although some lessons may seem hard, better to learn them here, than fall from grace as a senior leader. Each of the five characters mentioned were, in one sense, merely behaving in the way they had been programmed to. Their past learning gave them present power. Submit yourself to 'good programming' and make your mistakes while you can. When it is you at the helm and not someone else, it will not be quite as easy.

Four tests

As a young man learns and grows into a godly leader, he will be tested in many areas. There are four aspects of testing that I particularly want to focus on, ones that will refine the young man's ability to handle things on his own. They are faithfulness, faith, integrity, and character.

1. Faithfulness

> *'If you have raced with men on foot and they have worn you out, how can you compete with horses? If you stumble in a safe country, how will you manage in the thickets by the Jordan?'*   (Jeremiah 12:5)

Thinking back to the days of the local church where I was raised in Nottingham, I realize there were several priceless instructions that were given to me. One such instruction was a response to my request to preach at a mid-week service. My pastor told me, 'Prove yourself in the congregation first. I want to hear you pray, see you worship, operate in the gifts of the Spirit, and most of all be a regular in all the services.' Once a young man has proved himself faithful in racing with 'men on foot' and finds that he still has the strength to go on, even after being rebuked, corrected, and sometimes disciplined, he will be fit to race with 'the horses' on the day he leaves the senior man.

On 4 January 1809 a small French boy took one of his father's tools and accidentally gouged out his right eye. It also infected his left eye leaving him totally blind. However, he did not give up, but through persistence, not only gained a good education for himself, but sought to educate others as well. That little boy was Louis Braille, who became the inventor of the 'Braille' system so many blind people benefit from today. Are you faithful enough to persistently work for the good of your congregation, even though you may suffer personal hardship, so that no matter what life presents you, they will have a faithful servant of God watching over them?

2. Faith

Your enemies will test your faith. Even when, like Jesus, you are only doing good. The enemies of Jesus tried to get the former blind man to confess that it was not Jesus who had healed him. His response was the well known phrase, *'One thing I know, I was blind but now I see . . . '* Even your family can test your faith. When Jesus was about His Father's business it was His family that came to escort Him away. When no-one else can see the vision God has placed upon your heart, will you have the faith to see it through?

3. Integrity

When Absalom was on the run from his father David, instructions were given to capture him, but not to kill him. We are told that Joab and a messenger found him hanging in a tree by his own hair. The messenger was asked to kill him but refused even when offered a warrior's belt and a bag of gold. He would not do it even for a thousand bags of gold because King David had given an order. Joab however, killed him. This nameless servant was determined that he would keep his integrity, despite being offered a lavish reward. In the same way, Moses, although he complained bitterly about the people of Israel, never abandoned them. If a young man has learned all he can from his mentor he will be able to keep his integrity even when there are no onlookers to notice.

4. Character

There are seven wonders of the world in addition to the commonly known sights, that make up a character pleasing to God:

1. To love those who do not love you.

2. To keep giving when there is nothing left to give.

3. To serve and not be served.

4. To stand alone in a conflict with no support.

5. To accept the consequences of a bad judgement.

6. To take blows for someone else.

7. To keep a promise even when it hurts.

Again, if a man can prove himself of good character while under a senior man, he will succeed where others have failed.

> '. . . but we also rejoice in sufferings, because we know that suffering produces perseverance; perseverance, character; and character, hope.'   (Romans 5:3–4)

No-one in their right mind will enjoy having their character tested in this way, but with leadership there is sometimes an element of suffering to face, and it is not pleasant. And yet Paul states here that he could 'rejoice' in suffering. Let me explain how. Any man who wants to accomplish something will visualize the goal he desires to achieve and then work back from there, concentrating on each target that must be hit in order to progress to the next stage on the journey. Paul saw hope as his goal, but to get there he realized the first step back was to have character developed. In order to achieve character he realized that the next step back was perseverance, and one step before that was suffering. It was not the difficulty of suffering, but the realization that it was one step closer to the goal of hope that carried him forward. Just as a mountain is conquered bit by bit, so difficult times are endured and overcome, bit by bit.

Have you ever heard yourself saying: 'I need a break from the church, my wife, my children ... '? If God is the potter and we are the clay, then we shouldn't be surprised when we find Him applying pressure to a certain area of our lives in order to produce the finished product He intends. Being born again does not give you an anointing for ministry or serving, God simply took you out of the 'mire' and placed you on His potter's wheel. That is where the really valuable work gets done. Through the difficult times He is shaping and molding you, modeling perseverance that produces character and finally hope.

Every good planner will see further ahead than the present moment and work according to that detail. Suffering is only a means to an end. I am certainly not trying to paint a picture of hopeless depression and pain that will characterize you serving a senior ministry, but merely seeking to draw your attention to the battles of will, emotion, levels of faith, and most of all ambition, that will inevitably take place. Learn the lessons as early on as you can and take comfort from the fact that they will stand you in good stead to reach your destiny in God.

Chapter 12

The Apostle and the Apprentice

Whilst there are a few notable examples for us to learn from, the biblical relationship that probably reveals the most to us about the interaction between leader and apprentice is that of Paul and his protégé Timothy.

On their first missionary journey together, Paul and his companion Barnabas preached in the city of Lystra in Lycaonia. Theologians have pieced together enough evidence to believe that it was here a Jewess named Lois and her daughter Eunice were converted to Christianity. Eunice had a Gentile husband, and Timothy was their son. Although Timothy had been instructed in the Jewish religion, his Gentile father would not allow him to be circumcised. From their first meeting a bond of friendship developed between Paul and Timothy.

By the time Paul visited Lystra again on his second missionary journey, he found Timothy to be an active and highly regarded member of a group of local believers. Under the instruction of the Holy Spirit, Paul added Timothy to his apostolic team, and, since they would be ministering mostly to Jews, instructed him to be circumcised to avoid causing them unnecessary offence.

Paul visited Ephesus in approximately AD 63, after being released from his first internment in a Roman prison, and it was only a short time before he moved on to continue his itinerant ministry, leaving Timothy in charge of the church there.

One year later Paul wrote his first pastoral epistle, 1 Timothy, to his young disciple, who was struggling to stamp out a number of doctrinal errors that had crept into the church. Paul gives Timothy plenty of fatherly advice on this and a host of other practical issues. In order to gain an understanding of their relationship, and see how Paul guided this young leader, we will highlight some of the areas in this and Paul's second letter.

My true son

Paul identifies Timothy as his **true son in the faith** (1 Timothy 1:2) and also as his **beloved son** (2 Timothy 1:2). A young man in Timothy's position needs a great deal of affirmation from his mentor as he fumbles his way through his first attempts at leading on his own, and Paul does not hold back. He shows the depth of feeling he has for Timothy. It is indicative, no doubt, of the vast amounts of time Paul must have invested into his training, so much so that he is involved on both a spiritual and emotional level. This is something that many leaders would counsel against, and yet if a real relationship is to be developed, then there must be a high degree of trust, mutual understanding and respect, even affection, shared between them.

It is worth noting that Paul's letters to Timothy were **public** and not **personal** letters – in other words they would likely be read by the whole church. (The word 'you' in 2 Timothy 4:22 is plural, not singular.) Paul's affirmation of Timothy then takes on a new meaning. It wasn't just for Timothy's benefit, but the church's also. It is as if Paul is saying to the church, 'Look, I believe in this young man; he is my successor, chosen by the Lord.'

Boundary stones

Paul lives by the principle of 'boundary stones' that we have already discussed in Chapter 5. He reminds Timothy to faithfully observe the doctrine that he, Paul, has already laid for the church (1 Timothy 1:3–6) and encourages him that the simple truths of the gospel be continually reinforced. Whilst a young man may feel he has some 'fresh' revelation to share with the congregation (and he may well have), he will likely find that the congregation needs reminding of basic truths again and again. It has been said that a group of people working towards a common aim, need reminding of their core vision approximately every three months – the same seems to apply to core doctrine.

Wisdom on appointing leaders

Paul gives Timothy some guidelines on establishing a solid church leadership structure. It may well be that after a young man takes on the role of senior leader, that his mentor is 'called in' to provide advice and help where needed. This is legitimate and often appropriate, especially in the early stages. It should in no way be seen as diminishing the younger man's authority. Situations that may have seemed routine whilst the senior man was in charge (and ultimately responsible), can seem very different when viewed from 'the other side of the fence'. This is where the senior man's experience counts for a lot. In our example, Paul is giving Timothy a list of tried and tested criteria for electing leaders that he knows will stand him in good stead. No matter how much flair or potential a prospective leader shows, Paul knows that (especially in the light of the present proliferation of false doctrine) Timothy needs solid, reliable men of godly, refined character to strengthen his team.

Wisdom on dealing with people

In no other place would you find such an amazing cross-section of society than the Church. Where else would taxi-drivers, accountants, policemen, doctors and road-diggers rub shoulders? It is also an organization with a tremendous age-range. Paul gives Timothy advice on dealing with the various groups of people he will have to deal with: older people, young people, widows, church-appointed leaders, servants and masters. For example, he tells Timothy (who was obviously quite young to be the senior leader of a church) to respect the older men. If any one of them should need correction, he should take the man to one side and have a private word with him, not rebuke him publicly.

In the mix of advice on running the church, Paul also

includes plenty of exhortation aimed personally at Timothy. He seems to be sometimes gently coaching him, and at other times shouting at him! But it is all designed to encourage him to live a godly life. This is the point we should all take note of. What good is it to have read and disseminated all the books on leadership available, be a master of management techniques, and an endless source of new ideas for the church, if we disqualify ourselves (in Paul's language) from the race by not living a godly life? The success of our ministry will hinge, not on how much we know, but on how much we know God! All our teaching, preaching, praying and ministering should stem from our intimacy with Him. If we haven't got that, we haven't got anything.

Paul's advice to Timothy can be summarized as follows:

1. **Fight the good fight**. Paul reminds Timothy of the prophetic words spoken into his life (an effective mentor will always encourage his 'sons' to sharpen their gifts), and exhorts him to live a faith-filled life and to continually battle against false doctrine.

2. **Pray**. Paul urges Timothy to have a powerful prayer life. He wants him to be a man of constant prayer; praying for all men (1 Timothy 2:1) and praying especially for those in government.

3. **Be godly**. In a climate where many had gone astray from the true gospel, following various sects and factions – probably due to an area of doctrine they found hard or uncomfortable – Paul counsels Timothy to keep instructing the people about the truth that Timothy himself has carefully observed (1 Timothy 4:6). The emphasis is firmly placed upon **living a godly life** before **teaching a godly life**.

4. **Be an example**. In one of the most wonderful and at the same time daunting scriptures in the Bible for young men, Paul encourages Timothy,

   > *'Let no one despise your youth, but be an example to the believers in word, in conduct, in love, in spirit, in faith, in purity.'* (1 Timothy 4:12)

Yet again Paul reinforces the need for teaching the basics (v. 13); he exhorts him to keep using his God-given spiritual gifts (v. 14 and see also 2 Timothy 1:6); he tells him to give himself wholeheartedly to God's work (v. 15); and he tells him to live what he preaches (v. 16).

5.   **Keep pure.** Timothy is reminded to avoid those things that *'draw men in destruction'* (1 Timothy 6:9 NKJV) and to retain a clear conscience. Above all he must pay careful attention to *'guard the faith'* and flee youthful lusts.

6.   **Stay strong.** Paul also reminds his young protégé that all his work will not be 'plain sailing' and that there will be hardships to endure on the journey – difficulties to be dealt with. He is not dealing in specifics here, but merely giving his student a realistic outlook to save disillusionment later (2 Timothy 2:3–10; 3:1–9).

7.   **Study the Word** (2 Timothy 2:15). Timothy is counseled to commit himself to regular personal study in order that he might learn to *'rightly divide the word of truth.'* Every young man should learn to be diligent in his personal life and walk with God. Hymenaeus is mentioned in each of Paul's letters to Timothy as one who, after starting out well, had gone off the rails. He apparently came to believe that the resurrection had already taken place and was leading others astray with this false doctrine. This is why Paul is so determined that Timothy should study the word and keep teaching the basics.

8.   **Preach the Word** (2 Timothy 4:1–5). Paul hopes that the result of Timothy's diligence will be that he will be ready *'in season and out of season'* – in other words **at all times**. *'Convince, rebuke, exhort, with all longsuffering and teaching,'* Paul tells him, and instructs him not to try to 'tickle the people's ears' by telling them just what they would like to hear.

We are not told very much of how Timothy responded to Paul's instruction. What he thought about it, how he felt, whether he found it easy or difficult to do what he was being asked. But Paul seems to me to be the exemplary mentor. Loving and gentle, but also firm, occasionally stern and to the point; always giving praise; always giving encouragement, direction, guidance. Above all Paul never puts the authority he has delegated to Timothy in jeopardy. Maybe when Timothy made a mess of things he would tear a strip off him in private, but publicly he always affirms Timothy before the whole body of believers as **my beloved son**.

Chapter 13

Giving a Bride Away

In this chapter I want to examine what happens when the time comes for a mentor to step aside and let his apprentice take the lead. It is a time of charged and mixed emotions for the senior man, and I would like to explore the feelings that he may have during this time. Remember, that whilst you are experiencing a huge change as you assume responsibility for leading the church, the senior man is also undergoing a major life change too. After years of having the final say on all matters, he must now function in more as a 'consultant' than a 'director'. If the leadership transition is to be effective, he must be prepared to let go and give you some breathing space.

When a senior man gives his church over to a man who has served him under God, for him it is like giving away a beautiful daughter that he has raised over many years. He may have been the one who had to believe God in faith for the finances to purchase the current premises, and all that was needed to accomplish the vision as revealed to him, not to mention the years of routine pastoral work that he faithfully carried out with his congregation. He can look at the building and remember when it was just a field or a much smaller edifice. Not only that, he can probably also look at each section of the building and remember each member of his congregation who worked as a volunteer – painting, fetching and carrying. He may have even laid some of those members to rest, commending their hard work at their funeral, and recalling all they did to serve the Lord.

He will be able to look from the pulpit after the congregation has gone home and still see the familiar faces of those whom he has loved and pastored over the years, through various trials and difficulties. Over by the baptistry he will be able to tell you of those he had the privilege of plunging beneath the water, after they had confessed their sins. Looking at his office he will remember the solitary times of prayer when he felt all alone in leading the church, hours when he waited patiently before the Holy Spirit while preparing ministry for his flock, and times when there were conflicts with strong personalities that tried, but failed, to destroy his reputation in the community. He will look out of the window to the car park or roadside and remember all the faces that came and went to their respective transport after a meeting. Most of all he will remember the times when he himself took the pulpit every week to pour out that which the Holy Spirit had poured into him.

Now imagine how this man will feel, handing this carefully nurtured church over to you? I have been in the position like many men, of being alone with the father of the one you want to marry, to ask him out of respect for her hand in marriage, and with the hope of receiving his blessing. The father's heart is torn in two – part of it saying 'yes' and part of it saying 'no'! If his feelings do not show at that moment, they probably will as the wedding plans are made and the day of the wedding approaches. He may give you many instructions concerning what you will have to do in order to keep his daughter happy – maybe telling you things that concern a little girl, not the woman that you want to marry!

When your mentor gives you the church he has raised, he will not see it in the same way as you do. Your feelings will be more impartial, because you are largely unaware of the past, but full of intent for the future, just like asking him for his daughter's hand. The next step of the vision will not be on his heart because God has given that to you. As a young man, about to assume responsibility for the church you need to be wise and respectful towards the feelings that will wrench his heart. If you show respect to your spiritual father, like honoring your natural father and mother, it will go well for you and prolong the days of your ministry.

The honor of grey hair and the glory of strength

There is a practice that God delights in that is sadly not as commonplace as it should be. When the senior man resigns his church to you, it should **never** be the last time he gets to minister to the church. I am talking primarily here about a situation where the senior man has moved on to accept a new pastorate or perhaps planted another church to 'start over' again. At least once a year, on the anniversary of its inception, the senior man should be invited to come back and occupy the pulpit once more. After he has ministered the offering should be embarrassingly great, and all his needs for that day or weekend should be taken care of in a 'five-star' way.

Even a senior man that has perhaps not given up the reins as easily as he should have in the final years, should still be afforded recognition as the man who served before you. If this has been the case, it may be wise to carefully consider any invitation to return to the pulpit, as it could do more harm than good, but it is to be hoped that any man who has heard God clearly about equipping and releasing the next generation will hand the church over with honor and dignity, despite his personal attachment.

Look at the example of the Philippian church and its founder the apostle Paul. The church did not consist of a great number of people, and they were, like any other church, far from perfect. However, one of the key principles they had grasped was to honor the man who planted the church from just a handful of women by the river.

> *'Yet it was good of you to share in my troubles ... not one church shared with me in the matter of giving and receiving, except you only ... you sent me aid again and again when I was in need ... I am amply supplied, now that I have received from Epaphroditus the gifts you sent. They are a fragrant offering, an acceptable sacrifice, pleasing to God ... And my God will meet all your needs according to his riches in Christ Jesus.'* (Philippians 4:14–19)

These scriptures make it clear that, whatever other problems the Philippian church had, the issue of honoring their founder was not one of them. From this passage we learn several key principles that returned the blessing of God to them:

1. The church took an interest in the senior man's future work – even though he had himself moved on.

2. They wanted to be involved by way of financial support, and that not just a token but more than their founder needed – it was a generous gift.

3. The church was not interested in what the other churches Paul had planted were doing, so much as they were interested in the man himself.

4. The church did not send a gift just once, but again and again.

5. What the church did was pleasing to God.

Because of their continued support for Paul, he responds by telling them,

> '...I always pray for you ... I have you in my heart ... I long for all of you with the affection of Christ Jesus...'
> (Philippians 1:3–11)

When the church remembers its pioneers or those who served it for a good length of time, the devil has no foothold in the vision of the church.

In order to bring balance to the right and proper honoring of the former leader, remember that you are the new man whom God has called to bring a fresh vision for the church and to build upon the work of your predecessor. You must honor the previous man, but you cannot continue to be led by him. It is no easy task to hold down this relationship of honor, whilst seeking to forge ahead in a new release of God's power – it takes work and sacrifice, as the church in Philippi found out. Their attitude was not merely political posturing – saying the right things, dropping hints in a newsletter that they supported the Apostle Paul – it was an attitude in their spirit that led to positive action. In no other epistle does Paul sign off with the benediction of *'The grace of the Lord Jesus Christ be with your spirit . . . '* except this one. He was clearly grateful for all they did.

If you are secure in the calling of God and the place where He has put you, then honoring the previous leader as he hands over his church to you, will only add to your anointing and increase your gifting. But, if you are insecure and feel the need to protect what you have by exerting your authority, then honoring the man will be a great difficulty for you. Remember that it pleased God when the church blessed Paul. There is an oriental proverb that for me illustrates perfectly the difference between secure and insecure leadership. It says,

> 'A man who knows not and knows not that he knows
> not, is a fool, so ignore him.
> A man who knows and knows not that he knows, is
> asleep, so wake him up.
> A man who knows not and knows that he knows not,
> is humble, so teach him.
> A man who knows that he knows that he knows, is
> secure, so follow him.'

Another story I once heard also illustrates the principle of properly honoring the senior man when he has given you his church to care for:

A man had a son who worked alongside him in the rice fields as a boy, learning the simple but vital art of irrigation in a dry and barren land. As the boy grew, he could not understand why his father did things in a certain way – dividing the water supply to flow into two fields – when to him it seemed that all his father needed to do was let the water flow into one field, bringing a better crop at a faster rate. For years the boy held this thought to himself without making any inquiry of the wise old man. The day came when the boy became a man and the father moved away to work on other things he had planned for his retirement. Without just abandoning him, the father made provision for his son – to a standard he himself had never enjoyed – and assured him of his advice if needed. The young man however, could only think of instant success as he surveyed the fields. In his thoughts he recalled the questions of many years ago. Now he had the authority to make the decisions, he would cut off the supply of water that irrigated the two fields and let it flow into one at a time.

As the seasons passed he observed that the fields produced a diminishing amount of crops, even though he gave them equal water, although not at the same time. His father returned for a visit to find all his hard work of the previous decades ruined, never be retrieved. His last words to his son were these, 'You may not see the stream of water that is constantly flowing every day under the ground, but it serves to keep the field alive and growing. The day you cut off the supply to do something impulsive was the day you drained the life from what could have been greater than anything I ever grew.' If that young man had left the foundations alone but built on them as he should, his success would have been great.

The young man in the story should have asked his father as many questions as he could about his methods while he was with him. Why did he do things this way? He could have also presented his own ideas and received the benefit of his father's wisdom as to why they would or would not work. He who ceases to learn, ceases to grow. Without even examining the reasons his father had, the young man decided he knew better. It is all about experience.

Which way are you looking?

In summary, look at the past with a grateful heart, but not with nostalgia, or the vision will never grow and move on into the area God intends. Looking at the past is not necessarily a problem, it just depends on how you are looking at it. You must at least be aware of the past, and you must show honor to your 'father' in the faith for his tireless devotion to the cause of building the church under God. Remember Lot and his wife? When they were moved on from the place where they were, they were specifically asked not to look back:

'Don't look back, and don't stop anywhere in the plain.'
(Genesis 19:17)

Have you ever considered why Lot's wife looked back at the place God had chosen to destroy? Was it her curiosity? Did she forget something? Did someone call out her name (whatever it was!)? Or was it to have a last look at the past with nostalgia, reminiscing for a few moments about what it was like and how it used to be? I am convinced it was the last of these. Rather than this, seek to honor the heritage that has been passed on to you by your father in the faith, focus on the vision God has given you and look forward with hope.

Chapter 14

From Generation to Generation

A different generation requires a new style of leadership. In the case of Moses and Joshua we see the prime example of a changing people and consequently, a changing leadership. We can summarize the ministry of Moses by saying he was the 'Leader of the Red Sea Generation', while Joshua was the 'Leader of the Jordan Generation'. The people they led had the same name of 'Israel' and yet were different in many ways – the most obvious being that Joshua's generation heard of the things that the Lord had done for their nation second-hand, rather than having first-hand experiences. Those who Moses led experienced themselves the exodus from Egypt and saw with their own eyes the wondrous ways in which the Lord used the ten plagues against the greatest nation of that time and caused their downfall in the Red Sea. Joshua's generation knew of these things as actual events by word of mouth, but not by experience. (In this brief summary of the two generations I am referring to the experience of adults, not infants.)

Similarly, if today you are a young man serving a senior leader, it is likely that he will have served his 'apprenticeship' in a post-war culture and will have taken on-board the prevailing attitudes and norms established in society throughout the aftermath of the Second World War. This means that, although it doesn't seem as if there are a great many years separating you, culturally and generationally there may be a huge divide – especially in the area of values, attitudes and methodology.

During his apprenticeship, the senior man whom you now serve would have been learning all he could, adopting the

methods and ideas of the one he served with a few modifica-
tions in order to fit the climate of his day. However, we are
now living in a time where the average young adult family,
where the parents are of approximately 40 years of age and
below, have little recollection or understanding of the
post-war culture, other than that which the media chooses
to portray. People have more, and on the whole, enjoy
more, compared to their predecessors. This generation is
comparable to the Jordan generation that Joshua led when
succeeding Moses.

In order to be relevant to this 'Joshua' generation, the
Church as a whole must be prepared to make some adjust-
ments to their approach. If I was to look into the bathroom
mirror first thing in the morning and see the reflection of
someone else there would be a problem! In the same way, if
the reflection of the local church is not seen in the community then that body is out of touch with a changing society.
The reason why it is so important that young men are trained
into the ministry, is that no-one understands the present
generation as well as those who are born into it. When older
people try to act like they belong to your generation, it's
embarrassing usually, isn't it? The fact is that God's plan is
for one generation to hand the baton on to the next, so that
they can run faster and further than we ever did. We must
not to try to hold on to the baton and run someone else's leg
of the race! It contravenes God's natural order.

God is preparing your successor

In chapter 34 of 2 Chronicles we are told the story of Josiah, a
young man who made a big difference. Verse 8 of the chapter
tells us that, *'Josiah was eight years old when he became king...'*
It must be a daunting thing to become a king at the age of
eight, but nevertheless, according to his royal lineage and the
customs of his day, this boy took the throne to the kingdom
of Judah. Whether he actually 'ruled' as such a young age is
debatable, but as the sixteenth king of Judah he inherited ten
thousand square miles of territory east of the Dead Sea
including Jerusalem with its temple. When God ordains a
man to rule His people for a moment in history it is never an

accident. God always prepares His leaders well in advance. It is highly likely that, somewhere, God is preparing the person who will succeed you – even though you have hardly begun your own ministry! There are some already ordained by God to serve His Body that may not be out of infant school yet!

On Monday, 18 March 1968 at 4.30 pm I was born and given the surname 'Fox'. Although a joy to my parents, I could not yet communicate, walk, talk, use the bathroom, eat by myself, or make any cohesive contribution to the life of the family. Despite all these inadequacies, it did not stop me from inheriting the name 'Fox'. In the same way, our God-given purpose dwells within us in seed form from the very moment we are born – quietly germinating until the day we become 'born again' and a new life and destiny open up before us, presenting us with everything heaven can afford. From then on, day by day, by faith we discover more and more about our destiny. Josiah, at the age of 8, no doubt understood little about the office to which he had been called. Neither do we, as we begin our adventure of serving God and following His Son, Jesus Christ, but if we follow faithfully and listen for His voice, the bigger picture of God's purpose for us will become clear.

The question of maturity

'In the eighth year of his reign while he was still young he [Josiah] *began to seek the God of his father David.'*
(2 Chronicles 34:3)

Many senior men will tell you that maturity does not necessarily come with age. Reading the full context of the two books of Chronicles leaves no question that the governmental administration at the time of Josiah's coronation had achieved little. To whom was God looking to bring about His purpose? An administration who had not done anything of significance in either the past or the present, or a young man? His father Amon had done nothing, his grandfather – Manasseh – may have 'put away' the national idols, but it was left to Josiah to destroy them.

At the age of 16 he began to seek the God of his forefather David. There was no manuscript from Moses to guide him, as this was buried beneath the desecrated temple porch. The administration around him were old enough to know the law of Moses off by heart, but without any scrolls to read from Josiah only had his own sensitive spirit to help him commune with God. As he looked around the kingdom of Judah he realized that something did not add up. It was not until later on that we read the rediscovered law of Moses confirmed his actions.

Earn your stripes

> *'In his twelfth year he began to purge Judah and Jeru-salem...'* (2 Chronicles 34:3)

Josiah began to take action as proof of his convictions. Likewise, every young man will have to earn his stripes before he is taken seriously. In verse two we are told that Josiah earned the reputation of not turning to the right or left. Look at how God was able to use the obedience of this young man to accomplish His purposes in the land:

- Aged 8 – he was crowned king of Judah in place of his father Amon.

- Aged 16 – he realized something was not right in the kingdom and began to seek God.

- Aged 20 – he began to purge Judah and Jerusalem of all that offended God.

- Aged 26 – he had brought about a change and had restored things to how God intended them to be.

Josiah is a good example of a young man born into a situation where the previous generation had lost its focus and gone astray. He had no immediate senior that could provide a decent role model for him, so he had to go it alone. We would prefer it if there were a smooth transition from one generation to the next, but it is sadly not always so. Even this does not prevent God from accomplishing His purposes however.

Josiah and the man serving a senior ministry

If you are stuck inside a structure where something is not right, it may well be that God is raising you up to be in the vanguard of a move of His Spirit. The first port of call is the witness of the Holy Spirit in your spirit, confirmed by the Word of God, that action is needed. I am not giving license here to the maverick behavior of those who see only the faults in a structure and long to change something – anything! A young man who has established a reputation of not looking to the right or left, and with the ability to be strong and courageous regarding the purposes of God, will be well prepared to bring about the necessary change for the next generation.

Generation to generation

If we do not hold men like Jeremiah, Josiah, and John the Baptist up as 'special' people with an 'exception to the rule' call upon their lives, but see that in Christ, the moment we were born again, all that was accomplished by Jesus was also instantaneously made available to us, then we will be on the right track and better understand God's generational thinking. We will begin to see ourselves as a link in an eternal chain – godly leadership spawning each new generation. There are a good number of men serving a senior ministry that fail to grow for a lack of understanding of the role they are playing in God's plan, centering all their thoughts on 'their ministry' and 'their accomplishments'. However, a young man with a teachable spirit will grow and eventually succeed his mentor, and in turn develop, teach and train other young men to succeed him – from generation to generation.

Chapter 15

Defeating Intimidation

There are a number of ways in which you may be intimidated whilst serving another a senior leader – so many in fact, that they could not possibly all be listed here! They vary of course, from one person to another. One man may feel intimidated by being kept waiting for an opportunity to minister, while another may feel anxious through over-exposure. The story of Nehemiah serves as a good study of intimidation and how this key tactic of the enemy is used by him to distract you from your God-given purpose.

Sanballat the Horonite

As governor of Samaria, Sanballat had an interest in Jeru-salem through family connections. His daughter had married the grandson of one of the priests in Jerusalem. Sanballat himself was a Moabite in origin. Moab was the illegitimate offspring of Lot and his eldest daughter, a major reason for them being excluded from Israel. Whenever Israel was in trouble, Moab was never far away.

In any church you will find those who would try to intimidate you, distract you, and turn you against the senior leader. You may think that sounds very harsh, but we must be realistic about the battle we are in. The enemy is very often successful in turning the 'troops' unwittingly against one another. The vast number of different church 'streams' and factions bears witness to the fact.

We find in chapter six of Nehemiah that time was running short in the effort to complete the great work of re-building the city walls. Sanballat is desperate to distract Nehemiah away from his task and so he invites Nehemiah to the Plains of Ono, at least 20 miles away from the job at hand. There will be many times when your focus is distracted by the intimidation of those who want to hinder or control the great work you have to accomplish. Nehemiah refuses to be distracted, so Sanballat writes an 'open' letter to him making an accusation that could finish him completely.

> *'It is reported among the nations – and Geshem says it is true – that you and the Jews are plotting to revolt, and therefore you are building the wall. Moreover, according to these reports you are about to become their king and have even appointed prophets to make this proclamation about you in Jerusalem: "There is a king in Judah!" Now this report will get back to the king; so come, let us confer together.'*
>
> (Nehemiah 6:6–8)

The letter was 'open' so that the courier could read it and tell everyone. Similarly, there will be times when confidences are broken and your life becomes an open book for the whole church to read. It could be that you have requested someone to pray for your needs, but instead they have reported it to their friends and somehow the senior leader has found out! Such intimidation can be very depressing and discouraging, but it will prepare you for future confrontations. It should also heighten your awareness of your own speech and conduct, and help you to refine your personal integrity.

Shemiah and Noadiah

Shemiah the priest and Noadiah, a prophetess, were two people that confronted Nehemiah with subtle intimidation. Nehemiah records that *'One day I went to the house of Shemiah...'* (Nehemiah 6:10). We are not told why he went, or even if there was an invitation, but they obviously knew one another. It may have been nothing more than a casual visit by 'the leader' to 'the priest'. Unknown to Nehemiah, Shemiah had made a deal with Sanballat to betray him. The priest was hired to call Nehemiah into the sanctuary to hide from a death threat. Nehemiah, understanding the law given at Sinai, knew that it was only permissible for Aaron and his sons to enter the sanctuary, and replied, '...*I would not commit a sin by doing this'* (Nehemiah 6:13).

The question that falls at your feet is this, 'Are you going to be afraid or do what is right?' Has anyone ever 'prophesied' bad things that have changed your focus? Let me encourage you to turn a deaf ear to those who have been hired to subtly distract you.

Many times in Scripture we read of the powerful influence of the opposite sex – like Samson for instance, who could tear a man apart with his bare hands, and yet be totally pliable under the influence of a woman. Nehemiah had managed to resist intimidation so far, but it had all come from men. There are times when a woman can try the same methods as a man and make the difference simply because she is of the opposite sex. Noadiah was a prophetess who was not saying anything that had not already been said to Nehemiah by others. Fortunately, incredibly focused Nehemiah, in an almost casual way, dismisses her intimidation – seeing her for what she is, a hired hand of his chief distracter – Sanballat.

The devil is the father of lies and will try the same methods through different personalities to shift your focus, so that the job in hand does not get done. But thank God, like Nehemiah, you may not be a prophet, patriarch, or law giver, but just a simple person who hears from God and gets on with the job!

Tobiah the Ammonite

Tobiah was a man who had power, but no inheritance or right to the work of God. He had a Hebrew name and had married into the Israelite family of Shecaniah. They had a son who married the daughter of a wall builder called Meshullan. In other words, Tobiah was in the center of an influential family, a member of which was laboring right alongside Nehemiah. What a powerful man! He had a finger in every pie! Inevitably there will be people around you who think they have more right to be succeeding the senior man than you do – even if it is evident that they have no anointing for leadership. This attitude can be revealed in a variety of ways: 'I've been here longer than you,' 'I have more experience than you,' 'I know more about these people than you do' are phrases that your 'Tobiah' will use. The worst thing is that all these statements are probably true, but the one thing such a person lacks is the confidence in Christ and the anointing and authority God has placed upon you to function in this office of leadership. This precious gift of God far outweighs the earthly qualifications and experience of those around you.

We used to have an ivy that grew up the back wall of our home and eventually caused a structural problem. It found very small holes in the mortar and over the years worked its way into them, undermining the brickwork. Each individual branch could easily be broken with your little finger, but collectively they were almost impossible to remove. In the church you will find characters that have been there far longer than you have, and who are so well connected there is not a great deal you can do without their consent. If you address a matter with one of these individuals you are actually addressing a large network of inter-married families and run the risk of losing them all. I found this out the hard way some years ago – though through God's grace it became a better church because of the experience! The bottom line, as always, when seeking to accomplish any task for the Lord is: 'did you definitely hear from God, and did He give you some instructions?' If the answer is 'Yes' then no matter what anyone thinks, you should do it! I am referring here only to 'obstructive individuals'. I am not suggesting that you should blindly carry out a project against godly counsel.

Geshem

We don't know a great deal about Geshem, other than he had a great deal to lose, but everything to gain if he threw his lot in with Sanballat, Tobiah, Shemiah, and Noadiah. At no point in the diaries of Nehemiah do we find Geshem acting on his own, but always hanging on to the shirt tails of someone else. Has a member of your congregation ever said to you, 'Everyone thinks so' or 'Everybody has told me . . .'?

'Everyone' is usually no more than a small but very vocal minority.

All these characters of intimidation can be summed up in one of Paul's apt phrases:

> *'A little yeast works through the whole batch of dough.'*
> (Galatians 5:9)

The yeast of intimidation, however applied, can affect the whole church if it is not dealt with swiftly. It is your responsibility, like Nehemiah under God, to be wise, focused on your task and not allow yourself to be distracted. The fire that burnt down the mighty oak tree started with just a few dried twigs left lying around.

Chapter 16

Staying Focused for the Task

The ability to remain clearly focused and 'keep the main thing the main thing' is a rare commodity indeed, but one that is essential to cultivate for successful leadership. We have seen that fighting off outside distractions is one way of staying focused. It is equally important to avoid looking constantly inward at your own performance and over-criticizing, or paying too much attention to the opinions of others.

Getting nowhere fast

King George III had a son called Fredrick Augustus, Duke of York and Albany. He was a British field commander who had such a bad track record that his contemporaries wrote a rhyme about him that is still commonly sung by children today:

> 'The grand old Duke of York,
> he had ten thousand men.
> He marched them up to the top of the hill
> and marched them down again.
> And when they were up they were up,
> and when they were down they were down,
> and when they were only half way up,
> they were neither up nor down.'

He was a man who would often be only half way to completing his task when the enemy hit him so hard he was knocked back to where he started from. As someone serving a senior ministry, you may feel from time to time that you are getting nowhere fast as well, but constant navel-gazing is not the answer.

The ships'that traveled from England to Australia some 100 years ago would reach a place on their voyage where they were required to circumnavigate deadly capes located exactly half way between the start and the finish of their trip. At this point it was either life or death for them and in the same way, a young ministry must use wise navigation if it is to avoid being shipwrecked on rocks that could be avoided.

Don't worry

Baloo the bear in Walt Disney's film *The Jungle Book*, sang about forgetting your worries and strife. Without wishing to sound flippant or irreverent, Jesus taught the same thing, advising us not to worry about such trivia as what we should wear, eat, drink and so on. The English word 'worry' comes to us from the Anglo-Saxon word 'wolf'. To 'worry' carries the literal meaning of having a wolf snarling at you whilst you are trying to sleep – or, in our example, concentrate on the focus of your ministry. Nothing will destroy your ministry quicker than constant worrying about what others think of you and how you're performing. In the same way as intimidation, worry must be dealt with ruthlessly.

Don't be discouraged

> *'Meanwhile the people in Judah said, "The strength of the laborers is giving out and there is so much rubble that we cannot rebuild the wall."'* (Nehemiah 4:10)

According to Nehemiah's co-workers, there was too much rubble to deal with, and their defeatist attitude caused much corporate discouragement. It wouldn't have taken a great deal of thought to work out that if the walls were half built, then the rubble was half gone, but they only saw their 'problem'. What appears to be an advancement to you could

look like something else to your congregation. It comes back
to that old saying, 'Ask ten people what they think and you
will get ten different answers.' But don't be discouraged. The
important thing is, what is God saying to you?

> *'Also our enemies said, "Before they know it or see us we will*
> *be right there among them and we will kill them and put an*
> *end to the work."'*   (Nehemiah 4:11)

This kind of discouragement is so blatant that it almost
deserves to be ignored. The work of God is bigger than any
individual or church congregation will ever be, because
it is **God's work** and not **your work**. On that basis the
Lord will look after His servants who are faithfully carrying
out His commands and cover them whenever they are
threatened.

> *'The Jews who lived near them came and told us ten times*
> *over, "Wherever you turn they will attack us."'*
>   (Nehemiah 4:12)

This verse can be better interpreted, 'drop your tools and
come home'! The families of those who were not involved in
the work were themselves a distraction to their relatives
who were. The times I have left my own family on the
doorstep, waving goodbye as I travel away from them is
heart-rending in itself, but to have them become a pressure
that is distracting the focus of God's work would be soul
destroying. A healthy balance has to be drawn. No matter
how many people are ministered to through your work, if
your family are not your first priority then something has
gone tragically wrong. I do not know who has more tears in
their eyes, my family or me, when I drive off to minister
somewhere.

Invest your time carefully

Your time is precious and as a leader many demands will be
made upon it. As we have seen, your family takes priority over
church life. Let me also qualify that statement by saying that

your personal walk with God must take priority over **everything**. If it doesn't, you will soon run out of momentum and won't function well in any role. Steven Covey said,

'How many people on their death bed say, "I wish I'd spent more time in the office"?'

It's a question of setting your priorities correctly. A church congregation demands a lot of 'hands-on' working time, and sometimes it will seem disproportionate to the amount of time that they, as a church, seem to give back. But you must face the facts – this is the way it is. You will begin to understand that the complaints and discouragement that seem always to be aimed at you personally, are coming from a completely different perspective than the one you see. Life looks very different from the other side of the platform. As time goes on you will understand more and more about the people in your church, their needs, and their own personal problems that their criticism often hides.

Nehemiah was always prepared. He didn't even change his clothes at any time during the great work of rebuilding the walls. Each moment he was ready to be a fighter, a defender, or a workman – whatever was necessary.

'Neither I nor my brothers, nor my men, nor the guards with me took off our clothes; each had his weapon even when he went for water.' (Nehemiah 4:23)

Always be ready for action and stay focused on your task. Remind yourself of your God-given priorities as frequently as you need to, in order to keep them paramount. Don't worry, don't be discouraged, and above all, walk with God daily, tell Him everything and ask Him to guide you on your way.

Chapter 17

The Last Adam, Not the First

In 1 Corinthians 15:35–58 we find a description of the first and the last Adam. The first was man – created by God to dwell in Eden and look after it for Him, the last Adam is Jesus Christ. The potential that Adam had was wasted because of his sin. Adam's name is synonymous with the Fall, but we rarely give any thought to what he was like prior to that disaster. Please indulge me for a moment while we look at Adam a little closer.

A brilliant man

In Genesis 2:19–20 we read that God brought all creation before Adam for him to name, while the cosmic realm of heaven looked on, eager to see the creative ability installed in Adam, put to work. If we superimpose some modern-day statistics on this scene in Genesis, an almost unbelievable paradox is created. Scientists have estimated that there are 500,000 types of plant; 22,000 types of tree; 30,000 types of fish; 8,600 types of bird; 6,000 types of reptile, and one million types of insect. Look at what Adam did. He looked at all the varieties of plant life, examining their texture and color in order to derive a name for them. That made him a brilliant botanist. He did the same with each tree, every type of fish, bird and animal. We are not told that he named anything in the solar system, but he must have had an understanding of the glory that surrounded it.

Adam did not have a text book, paper and pen, computer database or any other reference for all of this vast information. He only had his own mind. Creativity must have flowed from him like fresh water with imagination and ability that was only surpassed when the last Adam, Jesus, walked upon the earth preaching the gospel of the Kingdom of God.

It is clear that Adam was an exceptional being prior to the Fall, but we tend to focus on his sin. During your time serving, you may have seen a thousand faults in the senior man and often wondered why on earth you were serving that individual. It can also work the other way around with young men and their senior leaders. They may see him as a brilliantly gifted person, looked up to by many, and they can be incredibly shocked when they discover flaws in his character after holding him in such high esteem.

There are two solutions to this problem: young men need to grow up and be realistic about how they view their mentor, and the mentor himself should endeavor to be real and dispel some of the mystery surrounding his own person.

The power of the last Adam is in the senior man

Reading through the New Testament books you will see striking parallels between Adam and Jesus. The word 'better' sums up everything that Jesus represents, compared to Adam. Everything about Him surpasses the first Adam. As Adam lay down to sleep, God made from his body, another body that was to be his bride. In the same way Jesus laid down His life, surrendering His body to God's purposes, in order that through Him, God might initiate a new body – the Body of Christ, His Church – and make Jesus the Head over it, just as Adam was the head over Eve.

Discerning Christ

The Apostle Paul took the church in Corinth to task over 'failing to discern' the body of the Lord during their communion times. The context here was that, whilst taking the communion meal, there was a great deal of selfishness and insensitivity taking place. The rich distanced themselves from the poorer factions of the church, and some even gorged themselves. '...as if you didn't have homes to eat and drink in!' Paul exclaims. Because of their insensitivity some of them were beginning to 'grow weak and sick' Paul says. There is a parallel here to the young man's relationship with the senior man. When the young man begins to see the bigger picture, beyond his own feelings and inherent self-ishness, and begins to discern the body of the Lord – in other words to be aware of Christ's presence in his mentor – he begins to grow strong and healthy as opposed to weak and sick. The ability to discern the attributes of Christ in this way is a key to serving successfully during your apprenticeship. Through it you will begin to focus on the positive rather than the negative. You will be excited about the things you both agree on, rather than drawn to the 'grey areas' of dispute and differing opinion. You will become united by your common goal, instead of divided by culture or methodology. Both you and your mentor have access to the last Adam, Jesus, who has surpassed and subdued all things, so when you look at the senior man, seek to find those qualities of Christlikeness in him and forget about the natural traits of the natural man.

He is the spark for your great light

Take a single lighted candle in an open field very late at night. You can only see about two metres around you, no more, yet it does not alter the fact that there is a great deal more to be seen. When the morning sun next comes over the horizon, compare its dimensions to that of the candle! It is 150 million kilometres from the earth, 300,000 times the earth's mass, 110 times the earth's diameter and ten times heavier than gold in density. When that sun rises over the horizon what do you see? More than two metres around you – in fact as far as your eyes can see! The senior man is like a candle, providing the light that will help to guide you in your present surroundings, but he will never be able to equal what the last Adam – Jesus – can reveal to you. Ultimately, we serve the last Adam, not the first. Christ is the source of everything we need in life. Throughout the journey of your training and development under the guidance of a more experienced man of God, remember, while **you** are concerned with reaching the destination, **God** is more concerned about what He can teach you on the way. He who stops learning, stops growing. Your time spent learning under the ministry of another may in one sense be just a means to an end, but the wise will see it for what it is: the chance to learn, grow, make mistakes, be corrected, spread your wings and learn to fly, and above all, have Christ formed in you.

A Review

There is no better way to excel in your ministry than to have served a senior ministry first. It will be a chapter in your personal history to look back on with gladness, as you become the senior man teaching those who will one day take your place. Be strong and full of faith, but most of all, be compelled by the Holy Spirit to lead by serving others.

We have taken a look at some of the aspects of serving a senior man from a personal and professional standpoint. If you are considering serving a senior man in his ministry, or if you already are, take time out to have a 'self-examination test'. Consider your motives and how you might react in some of the circumstances we have discussed. Allow the Holy Spirit to pinpoint areas where your attitudes need adjustment. I am seeking to reinforce the point, in case you didn't get it already, that your attitude as one being trained for leadership is probably more important than your ability. Gift without character is useless and directionless. God can work with humility, but not with pride.

I also want to re-emphasize that to be in ministry you need to have broad shoulders and a pioneering spirit. You could find yourself climbing mountains where no-one else has ever been. You may fall and have to be rescued a few times; you may suffer a few injuries and retain a few scars; but the mark of a true leader and pioneer is that he will already be planning his next assault whilst recovering from his last in hospital! It will not get the better of him, but he will get the better of it!

Once God has anointed you to lead, established you as a leader in your own right, and gathered people around you, a change will take place in you, and from that moment your relationship with your mentor will be forever different. The fact that you surrendered yourself to him and to God, means you will be well equipped to carry the work of God forward into the next generation. This is a golden moment, so when it arrives for you, humbly thank God that He has brought you thus far safely, and resolve to lead with integrity and honor before God into the future.

Appendix

Questions with
Answers from Key Leaders

To conclude this book I wanted to include an appendix of questions frequently asked by young men seeking to enter ministry. It is here to give a selection of senior leaders, who have mentored and developed a great many young men in their time, a chance to respond to these questions and so give us an insight into the mentor's perspective, because our story has necessarily been told predominantly from the younger man's point of view. It will also help us to capture the hearts of men of God more experienced than ourselves.

The respondents are: Gerald Coates (**GC**), Barney Coombs (**BC**), Alex Buchanan (**AB**), Roger Helland (**RH**), Rev. Eric Delve (**ED**), Peter Lyne (**PL**), and Bishop Graham Dow (**GD**).

What do you look for in a potential leader?

Firstly, they are hungry after God, dissatisfied with life as it is, are out and about either among God's people or the lost, and are seeking to serve and bless. Clumsiness, mistakes and even sins are not the problem, if they are teachable, moldable and relational. (**GC**)

I ask myself these ten questions:

1. Does he recognize that God has joined him to me and has given him to me to be trained?

2. Is he willing to become a team player?

3. Does he understand to some measure what are our family genes. And is he convinced that they are also becoming his genes?

4. Is he vulnerable?

5. Is he free from the curse of receiving correction as rejection?

6. Is he clear of self interest?

7. Is he risk taker and a self initiator?

8. Can he endure a measure of hardship?

9. Is he willing to be taught self discipline?

10. Does he have integrity? (**BC**)

Primarily a servant heart. (**AB**)

I look for passion for Christ, His church, and His cause – in that order. I look for their potential which should be packaged in humility and a teachable spirit. (**RH**)

I look first of all for intelligence married to enthusiasm. I want to know – does this person have the kind of eyes that look at the world and analyze it, understand and relate to it and respond with enthusiasm to the challenges it presents. If I initially see those qualities, then I look for the Three Cs:

- **Character** – is this somebody who is actually living the gospel which he proclaims?

- **Competence** – is this person able to do the job which I need done?

- **Chemistry** – does this person fit in the rest of the people in the team and, especially, can I work with this person? Without chemistry everything else is hopeless. (**ED**)

The word 'potential' is unfortunate in this context. The Church has been littered with potential leaders, often very gifted, charismatic people, who produce nothing in terms of long-term reliable leadership. The first quality I would look for is faithfulness. In the parable of the talents (Matthew 25:14–30), Jesus commends both the man with the five talents and the man with two in this way:

> *'Well done good and faithful servant! You have been faithful with a few things; I will put you in charge of many things. Come and share your Master's happiness.'*

(Matthew 25:21)

An excellent part of the training is to give the potential leader a small responsibility and see how they cope with it. **(PL)**

Vision for the kingdom, a personal prayer discipline and self-understanding, as well as a clear giftedness. **(GD)**

What elements are essential to a young man in a serving capacity to you?

A willingness to learn, to respect age, to develop wisdom so that they can do things differently to their mentors without being disrespectful. The person must also have an ability to represent their mentor. **(GC)**

Does he understand that all service is to be primarily unto the Lord? Does he take the trouble to serve in the way you prefer or does he serve you the way he prefers? Is his service the bare minimum, or does he go the extra mile and serve with a joyous positive demeanor? Is he a clock watcher or do you have to encourage him to take time off? **(BC)**

Above all, personal humility and the willingness to make sacrifices. **(AB)**

He must share similar values and vision, must be a team player, and we must honor and enjoy each other. **(RH)**

What I look for in all leaders – excitement about the gospel and the capacity for original thought. The last thing I want is somebody who is going to demonstrate his orthodoxy by running of a series of well learned doctrines by rote. I am looking for someone who will challenge and stimulate me through his originality and creativity. I am also looking for someone who can operate under his own initiative, but without being clumsy – initiative and sensitivity need to go together. (**ED**)

Along with faithfulness, I look for honesty and openness. Dr R.T. Kendall once said to me: 'Every man has his weakness!' I don't expect a person to be problem free, but I don't want to run into a minefield of unshared issues. There must be accountability and openness so that we can work through any difficulties. In all of this, a teachable spirit is essential to the whole process. James says:

> '*God opposes the proud but gives grace to the humble.*'
>
> (James 4:6)

In all of this, emerging gift and anointing will be important, but faithfulness, honesty and humility are indispensable. (**PL**)

Loyalty combined with the freedom to be himself and not copy me. (**GD**)

Do you want to reproduce yourself in someone or develop what they have that you don't?

Yes, and yes! You cannot fully reproduce yourself with another, unless you are into cloning. However, many of the marks and characteristics of one's disciples, are evident. So for example, if you look at the disciples of Dr Martyn Lloyd Jones, you will see many of the characteristics he had in the pulpit, in their own platform/pulpit ministry. Far from being negative about this, it is a positive. Do you remember when the religious people looked at Jesus' disciples and said 'these men have been with Jesus!' This was not a sentimental response but one of horror, for instead of one Jesus there were now a dozen of them. But having said I do want to reproduce myself in others, part of the relationship is to develop what they have and I don't. Noel Richards is a classic case here. Twenty years ago Noel drove me around, while I talked to him about life and ministry, the sort of music we could be producing in years to come, I would dictate mail as I sat in the passenger seat, and unknown to me he was watching and learning. Listening to my talks (the same talk many times over!), he then began to write songs reflecting the content of my talks. Over the years he moved from an apprentice (where he did everything from wallpapering my house, driving my car and at times tending my garden) to a worker where he began to lead worship and write some really good songs. Now of course all of these years later he is a master worker in his own right, with a Vision for the Berlin stadium in 2001, where I am now serving him to help make this happen. At one level you will find quite a bit of me in Noel, but he has his own personality, his own outlook and his own focus ministry and I have been privileged to play a small part in developing what was there already. (**GC**)

Whatever biblical principles I have embraced and walk in, these I would want to see reproduced in him whatever his gifting may be. Paul in sending Timothy to Corinth could say of him *'He will teach my ways which are in Christ'* (1 Corinthians 4:17). Much of me that gets imparted to him will come through osmosis and out of time spent together. Unfortunately, not all of this will be positive. However, I see my task is to draw out the grace gifts that God has placed in him and to ensure that he spends time with those of the same gifting as him and who have the ability to equip others. (**BC**)

I would rather develop something in the young man that I don't have. (**AB**)

I want to do both. It is not an either/or situation. I must empower others to be and do all God has called them to. Everyone has a unique contribution to make. However, I want to be in a mentoring role to impart the wisdom and experience God has given me. (**RH**)

The answer is an unequivocal yes, of course I want to reproduce in someone that God-given part of me which is of value to the Body of Christ and the world around. However, I do not want the person to become a clone of me; only to absorb the parts of me they find helpful in building up their personal life and ministry. And yes, of course I want them to develop what I don't have. If I can encourage them to develop what they have to serve the cause to which I am devoted, then the whole work will prosper and God will be glorified (and as the senior leader, the better he does the more credit I shall receive!). (**ED**)

Paul said: *'Be imitators of me as I am of Christ!'* What is 'of Christ' in me, I would like to see reproduced in the men and women I am training. It's important that they carry something of my heart and vision, but uniquely expressed through their own gift and ministry. We don't want spiritual clones! More than anything, I want them to run further than I have! (**PL**)

The second, obviously! (**GD**)

Does your wife, in your opinion, have to like the people who serve your ministry?

I place a great deal of weight on the perspectives of my wife Anona. If she didn't like somebody I was working with, my guess is that I would come to the conclusion that there was probably something amiss which I was blind to. Nearly all the people I am working with Anona likes or is more than happy to spend time with. (**GC**)

No! But she must be able to trust them and love them as brothers in Christ. Sometimes, even I don't easily like them. Some of them are not easy to like. (**BC**)

Preferably yes, but it is not essential. (**AB**)

Ideally, yes. We are one as we share a unified perspective. She also gives me balance and helps shore up my blind spots. (**RH**)

Not necessarily. Sometimes young men can be abrasive and may, in their immaturity, make it difficult for people to like them all the time. The one thing that is essential is that my wife must believe that he is the right person, God-given, and a blessing to me. (**ED**)

The language of this question is somewhat loaded! Jesus said:

> *'I no longer call you servants, because a servant does not know his master's business. Instead, I have called you friends, for everything that I learned from my Father I have made known to you.'*   (John 15:15)

The key division in the Church is between that which is institutional and that which is relational. Because we build relationally, if my wife doesn't like a person, it is unlikely that I would like them either. However, as with Jesus and the Twelve, there will always be people in a team that you have a closer friendship than with others. (**PL**)

No, but it can be hard going when she doesn't! (**GD**)

Would you take the advice of a younger man?

Yes, of course. Any leader should take advice from younger people, particularly if there is warmth and respect and care in a relationship. (**GC**)

Absolutely yes! But I would want to train them how to share their opinion with humility. I have been extremely impressed with a young man who is in the process of replacing me as senior leader in our local church. When he has a different opinion to mine, he asks, 'Do you think there might be another way of doing this?' This gives me the prerogative of opening the door to receive his contribution. Sometimes, British people have the unpleasant ability of coming over as rather haughty and opinionated. (**BC**)

Yes, if I thought he had the wisdom to give me advice. (**AB**)

Yes, and I have. A younger man can offer fresh and God-given perspectives. I am not 'above' a younger man, he is not lesser than me. (**RH**)

Definitely. The young men on our team at St Luke's are constantly coming up with better ideas than I have, and since I am a baby when it comes to technology I would be a fool if I did not take their advice in dealing with the Internet and other such parts of modern witness. On more serious matters, like ascertaining the will of God and finding direction for the church body, it is vital to listen to the younger men and take into account what God is saying to them. (**ED**)

An important ingredient in all relationships is the ability to receive as well as give. The person who cannot receive from others, old or young, should not be in leadership. (**PL**)

Yes, in his field of competence. (**GD**)

How much slack do you give a training leader?

This is a difficult one. Give a trainee too much slack, and they will just go and make loads of mistakes and a fire-fighting clear-up job takes place with frequency. If you don't give them room to make mistakes they become clones. Wisdom from the Lord, drawing on past experiences, and taking advice from one's peers are all helpful here. (**GC**)

A considerable amount. Enough to make mistakes and then receive a commendation for trying (**BC**)

> *'Where no oxen are, the manger is clean.'* (Proverbs 14:4)

We must always make allowances for men being headstrong and clumsy. (**AB**)

Lots. I can't assume he is further along in his journey than where he is. It is like parents and their children. The standards are still high but should not be unrealistic. (**RH**)

I tend to give a lot of leeway to the young men that work with me. Firstly because I know that they will do their best work if they do not have me breathing over their shoulder and asking them what they are doing every second of the day. Secondly because I want them to develop true Christian character and this can only come when people make their own mistakes and are responsible for their own ministry. Thirdly because I want to have peers who work alongside me rather than dependent inferiors who are always beneath me. (**ED**)

This would depend on the level of maturity of the person. A leader in training needs to be given a sphere of responsibility for which they are accountable, but which is not subject to constant interference. Nevertheless, it is important to have regular feedback. (**PL**)

I would give him full responsibility for his delegated areas of responsibility. (**GD**)

In discipling a young man, how close a relationship should you develop with them?

Discipleship does involve a measure of emotional involvement, proximity, and a shared life. But the most important thing for the mentor, is to know that this relationship cannot carry on in this form for ever. I go back to Noel Richards. Noel and I still feel very strongly that our futures are together, but because of our ministries, and the directions that we are going in, we don't see nearly as much of each other as we would like, nor as we used to. It is very easy in that situation to either become manipulative, or for Noel to become unhelpfully dependent on myself. Strangely enough, just yesterday I was saying to Noel's wife, Tricia, that when Noel and I were spending a lot of time together, I eventually encouraged him to be looking for advice on personal and family matters outside of our relationship. This is a safeguard for him and kept me from being unhelpfully involved in every aspect of his personal life, marriage, relationships and ministry. Now there is a healthy distance between us, Noel and Tricia are far more likely to open up regarding the difficulties pressures and temptations than they have ever been. It is important that the person being discipled doesn't end up locked-up to that person and discouraged and relating to a wide range of other influences. (**GC**)

If possible as close as a father would be to a son. He needs to see the real 'you', good, bad and indifferent. (**BC**)

Close enough for lovingly honed criticism to be given and accepted, but not so close that they become utterly dependent on me. (**AB**)

Close enough to foster a trusting and safe relationship but distanced enough to not create a false sense that we are 'peers' – we are not on an equal plane. (**RH**)

It should be very close. Much closer than most ministerial friendships. It should be like a father to a beloved son or an older brother to a close younger brother. Ideally their hearts should be open to one another so that if the time does come for the younger man to leave, I feel as though a part of myself has gone. (**ED**)

I have already commented on the importance of building relationally. This would involve being in and out of each others homes where possible. Travelling together, having fun, sharing the occasional vacation, getting to know each other outside of ministry related activity. In the Institutional model, people only meet at leadership forums, staff offices and church events. However, the depth of involvement will be determined by the importance of the relationship. (**PL**)

It can be a good friendship. Sharing your weakness is sometimes helpful, but it can sometimes also be very unwise – work on the friendship with discretion and integrity. (**GD**)

How do you know when it time to let a younger man take more of a leading role and you a lesser role?

I don't know! I probably have answered the question already. I have advisors, and they have helped me see things that I cannot see, maintain relationships with people I was going to let go of and release people I was hanging onto. I admit there is safety in a 'multitude of counselors'. (**GC**)

Bearing in mind that God's people are not there for us but we leaders are there for them. When I know he is spending adequate time in devotional preparation and that he shows respect for all those who have been entrusted to our care, and when I know that he does not have a need to be independent by proving he is different, and when I see the people responding positively to his leadership, then, subject to the leading of the Holy Spirit, I would feel a release in my heart to give him more authority and responsibility. (**BC**)

When in my judgment he is stable enough to do so, and when the anointing is so obviously on him that it would be folly not to allow him to do so. (**AB**)

When his potential to meet or exceed the required effectiveness becomes evident and when I have the confidence to release him with the responsibility based on a consistent proven track record. (**RH**)

I think this should happen as a gradual process. Even at the beginning of such a relationship there will be areas of professional skill where the younger leader is more capable than the older one. As the years pass, these areas will become more numerous, and as his gifts develop I give him more and more space; but it is important to bear in mind that competence and giftedness are not substitutes for a father-heart and the congregation definitely needs a father. The elder man should not relinquish that responsibility while he is still the main leader. (**ED**)

This factor needs to be programmed in from the outset, allowing for a gradual transition. The attitude of John the Baptist is exemplary:

> *'He must become greater and I must become less.'*
>
> (John 3:30)

Some will say that John's circumstance was unique as he was preparing the way for Jesus. Yet Jesus Himself similarly prepared His own disciples for a baton change. He said:

> *'It is for your good that I am going away. Unless I go away, the Counselor will not come to you, but if I go, I will send him to you.'* (John 16:7)

If we hold those we train in dependence upon us, they will never learn to be dependent on the Holy Spirit. (**PL**)

When he or she is ready to accept it and the body of believers already recognize it. (**GD**)

What is the greater need today, enthusiastic young men or fathers?

Both! Without enthusiastic young people it is impossible to father or mother them (and I am committed to women in leadership at all levels). On the other hand we have a lot of enthusiastic young people and no one to father or mother them. I am praying that the two will meet up! (**GC**)

If you change the term 'enthusiastic young men' to 'godly, enthusiastic young men' then my answer would be both! (**BC**)

Fathers. There are so few and they are so desperately needed. (**AB**)

Both are needed. 'Young men dream dreams while old men can kill them.' Young men need to dream while they also need mature fathers who will encourage, empower, and bless them. We must pass the torch on to the next generation. (**RH**)

Clearly it would be folly to oppose these two, but I believe the greatest need is for fathers. Most young men in Christian service are enthusiastic. Not all of them retain that enthusiasm and not many of them become fathers. We definitely need more fathers in the Church and more fathers who are prepared to love and train up younger men to become leaders alongside them. (ED)

The prophet Jeremiah, speaking of the judgement upon Jerusalem said:

> '*The elders are gone from the city gate; the young men have stopped their music.*'   (Lamentations 5:14)

For true health in the Body of Christ we need the dynamic cohesion between old and young, the synergy of wisdom and government with youthful energy and creativity. (PL)

Both are equally needed. (GD)

How would you approach the church body when the young man has made a public error?

Well, yesterday afternoon I was with a young man, a brilliant worship leader, in another country. He loves the Lord, has a tremendous anointing and is highly gifted. But he ended up in a long-term relationship with a girl which involved sex. When this was discovered their leader was keen to deal with this as privately as possible because of his profile in the church, the lady involved, parents etc. But within a few hours he knew he had to 'go public'. So the following Sunday he stood up and confessed his sin to the church. It released a great deal of forgiveness, he apologized to the girl, the parents, and has had to step down from ministry and is now in a regular job. My guess is that because this was handled so well, he will be back in ministry within a year or eighteen months. But he is going for counseling and developing a strong father/son relationship with the leader of the church. It produced a great deal of confession of sin at all levels, particularly sexual sin amongst young people in the church. (**GC**)

It would depend by what is meant 'public error'. If it is sin that requires him laying down his public responsibilities, he needs to be given the opportunity of openly judging himself. If he refuses, then this needs to be communicated to the committed church body. If it was a matter of handling something wrongly or speaking to an issue unwisely, then he needs to stand up, be a man, and admit his mistake. If he is not willing to take responsibility for his mistakes, he would not remain under my discipleship. (**BC**)

I would inform the church publicly, but in a 'Family Chat' session or some other less formal church meeting, and make it a learning experience for the whole church. (**AB**)

I would assume full responsibility as his covering and be as supportive as possible to him in the process. (**RH**)

I would encourage him to admit his error and apologize for it while I stood alongside him to make sure that everyone knew that there was no diminution of the affection or respect which I felt for him. I would also add my apology that the young man made the error while under my supervision and authority. (**ED**)

This would depend on the scale of the mistake. If it has far-reaching public consequences, then it would need to be handled publicly after consultation with the individual, but with maximum grace and redemption. If it is a relatively minor issue, I would prefer to handle this privately. The leader must avoid 'jumping in' when a mistake has occurred, particularly in a public setting, as this makes the apprentice look inferior. Neither should the leader quickly jump in with a judgement, but allow the individual time to give their own appraisal of what has happened. (**PL**)

I would take responsibility for it as far as possible and seek to protect him/her. (**GD**)

How do you handle confrontation with the young man?

There are of course two ways of confronting someone. You stand in front of them and wag your finger, which I find makes people defensive and reactionary, or you get alongside them, put an arm around them, and say 'I have discovered this – how can I help you?' It pretty well works every time. People feel loved rather than disrespected, supported rather than being left out on their own. Discipling others is the most painful but rewarding experience of my 30 years of ministry. (**GC**)

This would depend on the young man's personality. Generally, I want to know what is in his heart. What he says may be absolutely accurate, but his attitude could be awful. I try not to respond to his attitude until I have adequately considered his side of the confrontation. Frankly speaking, if a young man is constantly confrontational, I tend to withdraw. The kiss of death to our discipling relationship for the time being will be when I find myself withdrawing with weariness, exclaiming 'You know what, you may be right.' However, one thing I cannot tolerate is unmanly 'Yes men'. People who always agree with me, insult my manhood. One of my building principles is: 'Never build too much on an untested relationship'. Confrontation at some time or another is essential in order to discover whether your relationship is indeed, the joining of the Lord. (**BC**)

With grace and truth. (**AB**)

I try to assume the best, look at his heart, first ask questions rather than make judgements, give the benefit of the doubt, and then lovingly, gently and firmly confront with a view to his betterment. (**RH**)

Firstly I get somewhere neutral, alone with the person concerned, rather than weigh in with the description of his fault and ask for an explanation of whatever behavior should be dealt with. Then I would say what I feel and ask for his response. Having agreed a way forward I would expect us to pray together and embrace one another in love as a sign that the father/son relationship has not been broken. (**ED**)

Preferably privately, and at an appropriate moment. It should be done face to face whenever possible, rather than by letter or a telephone call. This should never be delegated to someone else to do. Always be responsible for your own issues of confrontation – don't be a coward! And always remind yourself of how merciful God has been to you. 'Mercy triumphs over judgement.' (**PL**)

Firstly the normal relationship should be one of encouragement and praise. I would prepare carefully, avoid overreacting, and see if the gently approach is responded to. It may be helpful to inform the person beforehand what the issue is so that they have time to think about their attitude. (**GD**)

Other leadership books from Sovereign World

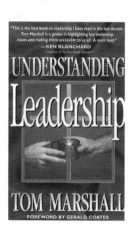

Understanding Leadership

By Tom Marshall

'*Understanding Leadership* is the best book on leadership I have read in the last decade. Tom Marshall is a genius in highlighting key leadership issues and making them accessible to us all. Using Jesus as the example makes everything come alive. A must read.'

Ken Blanchard, co-author of *The One Minute Manager*

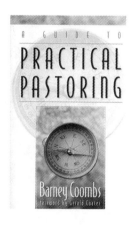

A Guide to Practical Pastoring

By Barney Coombs

If you are a leader, or feel God may be calling you to a position of pastoral care, this book is for you. It is full of wisdom, practical advice and principles. Whatever difficult pastoral issue you face, Barney Coombs' advice will be invaluable.

Apostles Today – Christ's Love Gift to the Church

By Barney Coombs

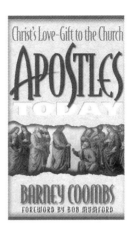

'Barney Coombs is a highly respected leader in the church today. This helpful and practical book is written out of years of experience and is a reflection on the meaning of contemporary apostleship.'

Dr Jack Deere, author, pastor and international conference speaker